Louis Aloisius Lambert

Ingersoll's Christmas sermon

Louis Aloisius Lambert

Ingersoll's Christmas sermon

ISBN/EAN: 9783741192067

Manufactured in Europe, USA, Canada, Australia, Japa

Cover: Foto ©Lupo / pixelio.de

Manufactured and distributed by brebook publishing software (www.brebook.com)

Louis Aloisius Lambert

Ingersoll's Christmas sermon

REV. L. A. LAMBERT, LL.D.

INGERSOLL'S
CHRISTMAS SERMON

REVIEWED BY

REV. L. A. LAMBERT, LL. D.

Author of "Notes on Ingersoll," "Tactics of Infidels," etc.

WITH AN INTRODUCTION BY

RT. REV. J. L. SPALDING, D.D.

AKRON, OHIO
CHICAGO   NEW YORK
D. H. McBRIDE & COMPANY
1898

COPYRIGHT, 1897,
BY
D. H. McBRIDE & COMPANY

INTRODUCTION

Oh, brother, 'mid far sands
The palmtree-cinctured city stands;
Bright white beneath, as heaven bright blue
Leans o'er it, while the years pursue
Their course, unable to abate
Its paradisal laugh at fate.
—BROWNING.

THE tendency of philosophic speculation, since Kant, is largely towards agnosticism and intellectual nihilism. It is maintained that we cannot know what anything is, for the reason that we know and can know only our impressions; whether they have a cause or what that cause is we cannot know. In all perception we perceive merely a condition of ourselves; and all knowledge, therefore, is a knowledge of ourselves. Nor can we truly know this self, for we are conscious only of its transitory moods and affections. We do not, in fact, know that we know; we merely believe that we know. We do not know that things really are, but suppose them to be. Truth, therefore, is not a harmony of ideas with things, but a correspondence of thought with thought. The critical philosophy, in denying the validity of inference from the subjective to the objective, denies that knowledge has any real value. We are forever shut up within our own self-consciousness, impotent to know whether there is an external world or whether we ourselves are anything. This criticism of knowledge, so far as it affects our views of the material universe, is simply ignored as senseless hair-splitting; but when it is applied to the spiritual universe, to God and the soul, many take it quite seriously and doubt whether it is not destructive of the very foundations of religious belief. It is impossible to persuade them that they do not know what matter is, but they accept, without much hesitation, a system of hopeless nescience as to everything which deeply and everlastingly interests the human mind and heart. They are ready to believe that criticism shatters all the priceless things to which men have clung — " The idols of metaphysics and the idols of religion; the idols of the imagination and the idols of history " — that it makes everything a lie: truth, honor and justice, hope, faith and love, freedom, duty and conscience. Much of the current scientific speculation leads in the same direction. It assumes that matter alone is real. The power, behind and within all phenomena, is simply the unknowable, that is, the non-existent, since intelligibility is co-extensive with being. There is nothing but force and motion. The universe is a machine which runs itself. It is, and the hypothesis of God is not needed to explain either its existence or its operation. Force and motion and their modifications are the sum and substance of all reality. Hence, human action is controlled by the same physical laws which keep the stars in the heavens, and a noble thought or a generous emotion is not more admirable or more praiseworthy than the feats of an acrobat. "The worst man," says Nietzsche, "is perhaps the best, for he is indispensable to the keeping alive of instincts and tendencies without which mankind had long since fallen into lethargy and decay. Hate, envy, ambition, and whatever else is called wicked, preserve the race, however prodigal and foolish the means. Whatever, in fact, a man may do or omit, he is probably a benefactor of the race." As knowledge is meaningless, virtue is worthless. Necessity is the only God and unreason is deified. In such a world life's true worth is lost. They who no longer have the power to believe in the living, loving God, lose faith in themselves. The only real thing left to them is matter, and possession is the highest good; money and self-indulgence are the highest aims. Apart from this, they are mere mental vagrants, who drift idly among all the great and vital problems. They are, indeed, still haunted by the Unseen, and hence it pleases them to listen to those who pass with an irreverent and mocking spirit, through the sanctities and infinities, from which the noblest minds and hearts have drawn hope and strength. In matters of the best and highest, the absolute and eternally real, they have neither faith nor knowledge, but, at the most, some sort of opinions, which they hold lightly, as being, in all probability, neither truer nor falser than innumerable other opinions which have been and yet shall be current. The existence of God, the reality of the self, the intimations of conscience, are interesting as questions of debate, as stimulants of thought, but not as subjects about which it is possible to know anything with certainty. They incline to believe that God is only a concept, an abstraction, just as truth, honor, duty, love, goodness, mercy, justice, science, progress, are abstractions. Thus the divine and infinite becomes for them a world of shadows. Their highest aim is to transform matter in every way. They think it a godlike thing to move rapidly, to live in splendid houses, to eat delicious food, to dwell in populous cities, to possess millions of money. They strive for a state of things in which they imagine happiness may be found, not understanding that happiness or blessedness does not consist in any possible static condition, in the possession of any conceivable thing, but in a ceaseless striving for the best, for truth and love. Righteousness, not abundance, is life. Fine clothes do not make the body strong and healthy; rich possessions do not make the soul great and free. "The highest type of man," says Aristotle, "finds his pleasures in the noblest things." Of such things money can never be the symbol or equivalent. It is a means, not an end. As thought and love unfold we perceive that they are more precious than all else; and thus we are led to understand that personal worth is the measure of all worth. What our Lord said of the Sabbath is true of all things. They are for man, not man for them. They are good and useful because they are helps to a right course of human life. Man is made for truth and love: the avenues that lead to God; and the measure of the worth of all institutions, political, educational and religious, is their power to bring men to the knowledge of truth and the practice of love. This is the measure of the value of every kind of human labor, the principle underlying all our social problems. The best climate is not that in which we are most comfortable, but that which is most favorable to the exercise of our noblest faculties, and the laborer is most fortunate not where he receives the highest pay, but where his work contributes most effectively to the development of character. Faith itself is not final; it is a means, not an end. When it is superseded by knowledge there is gain, not loss. Knowledge and love are final, because they are the highest conceivable modes of union with the eternal and infinite.

The misery of our age is the consciousness that what we live for is not God's truth; and that what it is easiest to turn to is still less His truth. We live without hope, not knowing, in the universal whirl, what to choose. We know that our way of life is not the best, that the things we chiefly desire are more or less worthless, and that we desire them only because we ourselves are poor and miserable. But this insight is looked upon with suspicion, we turn from it as from an evil suggestion; and plunge again into the world of appearance and show, for we have neither a mind nor a heart to know and love God's real world of truth and goodness. Those who have lost faith in God have no faith in ideals. But idealism is conscientiousness, and an age which does not believe in ideals is fatally driven to seek money and indulgence as the highest good. Hence our one virtue is thrift. The thrifty succeed; they gain wealth and honor, what matter if they make themselves unintelligent and incapable of the rational enjoyment of life. "The free life of God," says Aristotle, "is such as our brief best moments." Hence the high and free enjoyment of the faculties which make us human is the end of life, and the chief end of labor is to fit us for a noble repose and leisure in which the soul may play at ease amid the realms of truth, goodness and beauty. How far above us, with our inner poverty and vulgar show, our knowledge not for itself but for politics and trade, this pagan philosopher rises, sitting there where we dare not soar! To men who are not serious students, who are not seeking after truth, to whom hunger and thirst for righteousness is meaningless verbiage, who, having lost faith in the reality of the whole spiritual world, hang helpless in the network of material aims and desires, a frivolous and mocking critic and demolisher, like Colonel Ingersoll, comes with a charm and persuasiveness equal to that of poets and orators. When we deliberately walk in lower ways, it is pleasant to think that no man knows whether there be higher. After hearing him, they say to themselves: no one can know anything of God, the soul, freedom of the will, and human responsibility. The only thing we are certain of is that we see and taste and touch. Let us get money and enjoy ourselves. In humoring their religious doubt and indifference, he helps to confirm them in philistinism and secularism. In losing faith in God and in their own godlike nature, they lose the mightiest impulse to high and heroic life. "An immense moral, and probably intellectual degeneration," says Renan, in his latest book, "would follow the disappearance of religion from the world. You can get much less from a humanity which disbelieves in the immortality of the soul than from one which believes."

Everything depends on what we really believe and love. He who prefers alcohol to honor and duty is what this preference makes him. An infinite faith and hope have lived and still live in the world. These have been and are the wings whereon men have risen towards the highest and the best. To persuade them that their divinest and holiest thoughts and moods spring from mere delusion is to discourage and degrade them. The soul believes that it lives in God and with God. To destroy this belief and to make it feel that it is wedded only to matter, to what is beneath it, is to sadden and bewilder, to drive it forth from its true home into a desert where it can commune only with the senseless wilderness and beasts of prey. The union of the higher with the lower produces the lower. The mulatto, even the octoroon, is still a negro. He who would help men, must help them to believe that the beginning and end of all things is life, not matter. Of the dead as utterly separate from the living, we can have no conception; for by the very law of our being, we associate matter with sensation and sensation with life. Life, then, is within and around, beneath and above all things. Our notions of matter are all permeated with thought and feeling, consequently with life. Force, size, hardness, and whatever other ideas enter into our views of the material world, have meaning only when blended with what lives and thinks. Nature is instinct with mind, and if there were no Supreme Mind there would be no universe. In the universe there is a tendency from chaos to cosmos, from the dead to the living, from the outward to the inward, and this movement is Nature's revelation of God. Life, conscious of itself, is aware of its own immortality, for the highest consciousness is of that which, like truth and love, is eternal.

Whoever seeks to persuade men to lower views

of life, is a frivolous thinker, and his influence is fatally immoral. Only a great moral purpose can sustain a great soul, and a great moral purpose rests finally on faith in God. If there is no God, all that is, is meaningless and vain. If He is, I fear no evil; if He is not, I hope for no good. Plato's precept is — learn to die; Spinoza's — learn to live; Christ's — learn to know God. Death shows the vanity of life; true life shows the impotence of death to do harm to those who love God. He reveals Himself within the will of man as within his mind. We cannot even desire that anything but the Infinite Best should satisfy us, and, if we acted with full consciousness, we should understand that in all things we pursue, we seek God, however blindly; we should know that we can be made blessed, not by the possession of anything, not even by a virtuous condition of soul, but only by the living view of God's presence in the world. Whatever state we attain to, we value it as a means to something better. Shall we not then, at last, seek to reach the best? Or shall we believe that life is but a sickly dream? It is God who whispers within the human conscience, which is but a phase of consciousness; it is He Who puts morality in the nature of things; Who makes a high and honorable mode of iife, followed with perseverance, become, in time, a pleasant kind of life, while the immoral pursuit of power, or pleasure or money leads to misery. It is He Who causes noble and virtuous sentiments to give delight and courage to those by whom they are genuinely felt, whereas low passions make wretches and cowards. It is He Who makes virtue self-preservative; vice, self-destructive.

If the eye were not sunlike, how could it behold the light? If the soul were not godlike, why should it forever yearn for God, seeking Him, behind all that it follows and loves? Our highest aspirations reveal our deepest needs. Religion, then, is the greatest and holiest factor within us. "The thing a man does practically believe," says Carlyle, "the thing a man does practically lay to heart, and know for certain concerning his vital relations to this mysterious universe, and his duty and destiny there, that is, in all cases, the primary thing for him, and creatively determines all the rest." Whether or not man shall ever fathom the mystery of being, shall ever truly read Nature's secret, to believe in God, which in the past has been the highest wisdom, will in the future also continue to be the highest wisdom; and as we more and more realize that God is the highest truth, perfect holiness and infinite love, we shall evolve, not a new religious creed, but new and fairer manifestations of the healing, strengthening and ennobling power of religion — of that religion which is embodied in the life and teachings of Christ.

In the midst of all our feeble and bewildering scepticism, we see, more clearly than men have ever seen before, the hopeless disappointment and disgust which sensual indulgence involves. The thing has been analyzed and we hold our breath. The ideals of money and place the intelligent now recognize to be unsatisfactory; and we begin to understand that, to be famous is to survive only as an impersonal influence, to outlive ourselves in something which is not ourselves. What remains to us then but to be Buddhists or Christians, to aim either to cease to be, or to live with the Eternal? What is truth and love? I find fault with Colonel Ingersoll, not because his faith and opinions are not mine, but because he approaches the most vital and sacred subjects which the mind of man can consider in a frivolous and mocking spirit; because he discusses the most momentous and solemn of all questions, without reverence, which is the highest feeling known to man. "Look for a people entirely destitute of religion," says Hume, "and if you find them at all, be assured they are but a few degrees removed from brutes." This is the testimony of the most sceptical mind, whose thought has found a permanent place in literature. Since religion, of some kind, interpenetrates all thought, love and aspiration is part of all human nobleness and excellence, of all struggles for truth and justice, of all solace in wretchedness, of all hope in the presence of death. To combat it, in its highest form, with shameless assertion, sarcasm and ridicule, is to sin against human nature itself. "Ridicule is," to quote Carlyle again, "intrinsically a small faculty. It is directly opposed to thought, to knowledge, properly so called; its nourishment and essence is denial, which hovers only on the surface, while knowledge dwells far below. Moreover, it is by nature selfish and morally trivial; it cherishes nothing but our vanity, which may, in general, be left safely enough to shift for itself. . . . It is not by derision or denial, but by far deeper, more earnest, diviner means, that anything truly great has been affected for mankind; that the fabric of man's life has been reared, through long centuries to its present height." As it takes a hero to understand a hero, a poet to love a poet, so only a reverent and religious mind can rightly deal with questions of religion. We are offended less by what Colonel Ingersoll says, than by the spirit in which it is said. Marcus Aurelius, in the midst of dissolving paganism, is bewildered. He does not attempt to conceal his doubts as to whether there are gods; but he is always serious and earnest, and hence his thoughts are precious to all who think and feel, whatever their faith or lack of faith may be. We are aware that he is a man with men, who treats reverently whatever mankind has held to be high and sacred. Socrates drank hemlock because he was found guilty of blaspheming the gods of Athens, but the noble and religious spirit which breathes in all his utterances makes him not only the father of philosophy, but the brother of prophets and saints. For Voltaire, himself, it may be possible to find excuse, for he was by nature a persifleur, a man born to take a light and superficial view of all things, and to mock, therefore, at himself and mankind. Besides he lived in an age when religion had become associated with inveterate and intolerable abuses. And, then, he had wit and style, and not the mere faculty of caricature.

Fichte, the least orthodox of men, accused even of atheism, is always earnest and noble in his treatment of religion. What worlds lie between Colonel Ingersoll and him, who wrote these words: " Even to the end of time all wise and reverent men must bow themselves before this Jesus of

Nazareth; and the more wise, intelligent and noble they themselves are, the more humbly will they recognize the exceeding nobleness of this great and glorious manifestation of the Divine Life." Richter, I suppose, was not a Christian, but this is what he writes: "Christ was the holiest among the mighty, and the mightiest among the holy. He lifted, with His pierced hands, empires off their hinges; He turned the stream of history and He still governs the ages."

Colonel Ingersoll forgets that religion is not, in any proper sense at all, a subject for verbal warfare a question to be settled by a debating club. It is our very human life, our highest aspiration, our deepest need. It is a life to live, an attitude towards God and His Universe to be ceaselessly held, and only in a very minor way and chiefly for those who have lost the sense of its real import is it a matter for controversy and logic-chopping. As the faith of healthful minds in the reality of the external world is not disturbed by metaphysical theories, so belief in God and the soul rides triumphant over the arguments of materialists and atheists. Difficulties there are, many and possibly insuperable, but whatever line of thought we take, the moment we attempt to descend to the ultimate cause and essence of things, reason seems to be-

I.C.S.—2

come involved in hopeless contradictions. A universal unconscious principle from which all things proceed is as incomprehensible as an Infinite Being Who thinks and loves. The religious do not claim that they have a clear view of the object of their adoration. Their insistence upon the virtue and necessity of faith is evidence of this. They recognize that what is plain is the exception, and that mystery is everywhere. In the limitless expanse a few stars twinkle; all else is darkness. "There is a chain in the hand of God," says Max Müller, "which holds together all the beings of the universe, even to the smallest grain of sand. Here and there we discover its links, but, for the most part, it is hidden from our sight." Whatever our solution of the enigma of being and of life, we accept it on faith. No man can know that the unconscious can create consciousness. The atheist believes in his dogma, as the theist believes in his God. The one holds that the Infinite Power, which all dimly discern, is mere matter; the other is certain that it is life and truth and love and beauty. If the atheist ask, how could God create such a world? the theist replies with the question: How could matter create a soul which thinks and loves, which is nourished by deathless hope and uplifted by infinite aspiration? To those who affirm that the Almighty is fatal, blind and senseless, great human hearts will forever reply, with their cry of faith, that the infinitely strong is also the infinitely wise and good. If the materialist were right, those who believe in God would still have the better part. It is a higher human thing and a mightier, to trust the larger hope. We cannot but believe that the highest is more nearly akin to what within us is high than to what is low. The ship of faith is a Columbian ship. Believers have been world-compellers and world-revealers. They have conquered with Paul; they have founded empires with Charlemagne; they have written epics with Dante and Milton; they have read the secret of the stars with Copernicus and Kepler; they have sailed the sea of darkness with Columbus; they have cleared the wilderness for the people's rule, with Pizzaro and Cortez. Life's current has welled within them in a clear, perennial, fresh-flowing stream; and they have hugged death himself, believing that he unlocks the door through which we pass to God, by Whose throne flows life's full tide. They live the life, and the doctrine whereby it is expressed is for them nowise uncertain. The objector they find to be something of a trifler. He is not wholly in earnest about anything, else he would find less time to argue and dispute. This verbalism, after all, settles nothing that is worth settling. He who tells us what difficulties and doubts he has, and what difficulties and doubts the faith of others suggests to him, renders us no real service; and he is, besides, as uninteresting and tiresome to a self-active mind as one who complains and laments. Let those, who seek pretexts for doing nothing or doing ill, listen to him; but they, who feel that life is eternity's seedtime, dwell in worlds where all this phrasemongering is as unprofitable as the discussions of schoolboys or as a politician's zeal for the country's welfare. Why should the good and wise care to see a man pull even the most wretched thatched hovel about the heads of its inmates? Show them how and where they may find a nobler dwelling, and they will leave the hovel. Be a builder, not a destroyer; a creator, not an objector.

Colonel Ingersoll's method of criticism is one which cultivated men have long since thrown aside. The critic's function, as scholars now hold, is not to point out faults, but to discover and make known what is true, excellent and beautiful. What is trivial and hideous anyone may understand and see, but to learn to know and appreciate the best that has been thought and said, we all need the instruction and guidance of those who are wiser and more sensitive than ourselves. If he who teaches me a new truth, however disagreeable, is my benefactor, so is he who helps me to see what is fair and true in life and literature; but he who criticises the Bible,—of which Kant said that a single one of its lines had consoled him more than all the books he had read,—in the mood and temper of a mocker and coarse humorist, is to me like the bull with hay on its horn, mentioned by Horace. He is as interesting as Voltaire when he declares that Shakespeare has not the smallest spark of good taste or the least acquaintance with the rules. Colonel Ingersoll's controversial method is as unsatisfactory as his critical. He is a polemical guerrilla. He does not attempt to lay formal seige to the fortress of religious truth, but he lies in wait for some sleepy sentinel or band of marauders, and when he has fired his blunderbuss, chuckles with delight, as though he had gained a victory. No well-read man will claim that he says anything new. The significance of what he says lies in the emphasis with which he says it. Emphasis is bad style. It is the attempt to make poverty look like riches, to give to platitudes the semblance of profound thought. His secret is that of the rhetorician, who, when he has made a thing appear ridiculous, would have us believe there is nothing more to say. But even those who do not think deeply, feel, when they have read him, that there is infinitely more in the religion of Christ than any words of his will ever reveal. Sane men will never believe that life is a comedy, a mere freak of nature; and, consequently, they can never be persuaded that religion is a delusion. As time lengthens, thought widens; but the larger view does not annul the truth there is in the faith of those whose world was narrower. To think otherwise is to be a philistine; is to imagine, for instance, that the classical languages are dead languages, whereas, in truth, they are the living mother tongues of all who think and aspire nobly. In them there breathes the spirit of our intellectual ancestors — of the masters who first showed the world how to use the mind; which gave form and direction to philosophy, science, poetry and eloquence, and voice in the idioms of all cultivated peoples, the power to develop and inspire; and in which there is found neither the knowledge of nature nor the experience of life. The fundamental conception of Christianity is that of progress in the knowledge of God and His universe. The increasing intelligence of mankind is the gradual revelation of the Divine Mind. To deny this is to deny God and reason. All real progress, indeed, is the growing manifestation of the Infinite Being, Who lives and loves within the whole. He fulfills Himself in many ways, and the more we bring all our endowments into activity, the more like unto Him do we grow. The lack of the sense for historical perspective is Colonel Ingersoll's great defect. He projects our modern consciousness into the past, and finds fault with his great grandfather because he did not know what it was impossible for him to know. He is like one who should treat Columbus with contempt, because he sailed for Cipango and not for America, whose very existence was unknown to the Europe of his day. He imagines the Copernican system is an argument against inspiration. He assumes that the Bible is a book of science, and then points the finger of scorn at it because it does not teach the Newtonian theories. He throws himself into the primitive and barbarous life of the wandering tribes of Israel, and is scandalized because their moral code is not wholly comparable to that of a highly-developed and complex social organism like our own. There was a time when feudalism was a blessing; for us it would be a curse. There has been a time when a people could save itself only by expelling foreign and unfriendly elements; in the modern age this is neither necessary nor desirable.

Colonel Ingersoll believes in the theory of evolution,

and treats Christianity as though development did not exist. He makes humanitarianism the supreme and only saving truth, and refuses to recognize the fact that the Christian religion has created the conditions that have made such faith possible. He exalts the worth of woman, and fails to see that the power that made her man's equal before God, thereby set her feet in the way of a larger and nobler life. He extols freedom and forgets that the germ of our modern liberties lies in the apostolic appeal from man to God, from emperors and mobs to conscience, which is found in the separation of the spiritual and temporal powers, and distinguishes Christian civilization from all other. He is eloquent in the praise of true marriage and of homes consecrated by the heart's devotion; and he has only words of scorn for the Church which has ever set its face against polygamy, and has fostered with ceaseless care the virtue of chasity, which is the mother of pure love, and a woman's crown. He is filled with horror at the thought of wars and massacres in which religious passions have played a part, and he has no words of commendation for the army of Christian men and women, who, in every age, have walked in the ways of peace, have quelled strife, have spread good will, have redeemed captives, have watched by the deathbeds of the forsaken, have moved like ministering angels in the midst of the victims of pestilence and famine, and have stooped to breathe words of hope into the ears of the most abandoned criminals. "The only irremediable ill," says George Eliot, "is that which falls upon a mind debased." But Christ has taught us that the disease even of a degraded nature is such that the germ of the divine life is never wholly extinguished even in the most perverted soul.

I have reason to believe that Colonel Ingersoll is a generous and kind-hearted man. Let him turn from persecutions and inquisitions, from predestination and infant damnation,— since nothing of this is, in any true sense, Christianity,— to the religion of infinite hope and love, of gentleness and peace, of mercy and forgiveness, of purity and perfectness through suffering, which the Blessed Savior taught. Let him think of that charity which enters the darkest recesses of vice and misery, to bring light and healing; which weakens the barriers that separate class from class, and nation from nation; which carries into war itself the spirit of pity and humanity. Let him think of the tender thought which watches over childhood even in the mother's womb, which has made every true man and every good woman the lovers and helpers of those little ones, who keep the world young and fresh, whom Christ took into His arms and blessed, and of whom He said, their angels see God's face in heaven. Let him think of that wide sympathy, which embraces all tribes and peoples, all ages and conditions, which, while it seems to concern only the perfection of individual man, becomes the vital principle of civilization, giving new meaning to life, new strength to morality, new vigor to the nations, introducing into history a higher conception of God and of man, and of man's duty to God and to his fellowman, issuing in a purer and nobler worship, and slowly flowering into the fuller consciousness of the brotherhood of the whole race, into which the spirit of nationalism shall at length, as generous hearts believe, be absorbed. This religion of Christ has conquered where philosophies have failed; it has ennobled where arts have degraded; it has wrought for larger and purer life where republics have perished in sensuality and lawlessness. Its chronic vigor is so unfailing that the very diseases which find a nest in its constitution, seem to grow immortal.

"We understand ourselves to be risking no new assertion," says Carlyle, "but simply reporting what is already the conviction of the greatest of our Age, when we say that, cheerfully recognizing, gratefully appropriating, whatever Voltaire has proved or any other man has proved, or shall prove, the Christian religion — once here — cannot again pass away; that, in one or the other form, it will endure through all time; that, as in Scripture, so also in the heart of man is written: ' The gates of Hell shall not prevail against it ' . . . It was a height to which the human species were fated and enabled to attain; and from which, having once attained it, they can never retrograde."

The world, indeed, is still far from the perfect knowledge and love of the Divine Life, which is revealed in Christ. We are all still misled by error and passion; but when we look back we see that progress has been made. In the spiritual, as in the material world, great and far-reaching changes take place in long lapses of time. The enthusiast expects to accomplish in a generation what God takes centuries to bring about. He lacks insight. The wise will learn patience, and look less to what makes an immediate impression than to what leads to truth and permanent results. The important thing is to keep clear, within the mind and the conscience, true distinctions between right and wrong. We readily admit that untruthfulness, cruelty and dishonesty are vices; but we are slow to believe in the guilt of the indifferent and unbelieving. It is the fashion to make doubt a virtue, as though one could have the right to rest unresolved where vital interests are at stake, as though we did not live in a world where faith alone makes action possible.

"Belief or unbelief
Bears upon life, determines its whole course."

J. L. SPALDING.

INGERSOLL'S
CHRISTMAS SERMON

Reviewed by L. A. Lambert

❧❧❧❧❧

CHAPTER I.

To the Editor of the Evening Telegram:—

I AVAIL myself of your suggestion to reply to some statements made by Mr. Ingersoll in his latest outbreak. He has been comparatively quiet about Christianity of late years, and some began to believe his monomania had subsided; but it is very evident they erred in their diagnosis. Owing to his silence he had begun to fall away from public attention, which constantly seeks new and fresh stimulants. He was settling down into that condition which has been aptly phrased "innocuous desuetude," a condition not at all congenial to one whose thorax expands with applause. This may account for his late pyrotechnic display.

In his late utterances Mr. Ingersoll only threshes over again the old straw of his lectures on "The Mistakes of Moses," "The Gods," "Skulls and Ghosts." All these I have read, and in reading his last effort I recognize the old familiar faces of his sophisms, mis-statements and tricks of speech — the same venerable chestnuts that, unlike good whisky, have not improved with age.

The Colonel is growing old, like myself. The sun of our days is setting beyond the hills, and illumines only with cold, retreating rays the valley shadows that are closing in about us like a shroud. The tide of life's fitful fever is going out, and we are drifting out with the tide. And then? A question to be asked.

In his old lectures Mr. Ingersoll exhausted all the ammunition in his anti-Christian armory, and is now very naturally under the necessity of repeating himself. He is not to be blamed for this, and I do not mention it as a reproach. Few men can be original to the last. There is a limit to the most prolific imagination, and it has been observed of even the greatest writers that they wrote themselves out. Scott, Dickens, Thackeray, Hugo, the elder Dumas, and others, who lived beyond middle life, began to repeat themselves toward the last and it should not be expected that Ingersoll — equal in fiction to any of them — should prove an exception to the rule. It is expecting too much. We should take the best he can give us with thankfulness, and remember the old Irish fiddler who knew but two tunes. When requested to play he would ask: "*Which* 'l you have?" With the doughty Colonel when attacking Christianity, it is a question of *which* 'l ye have, Moses, Skulls, Gods, or Ghosts, or will an *olla podrida* of tidbids from all of them do? But whichever he may grind out, there is always a monotonous sameness of grind that is suggestive of a perambulating crank organ.

The only objection that one can reasonably urge to these repetitions is that they put one to the tiresome necessity of repeating the same refutations with the same music-box regularity, and then it becomes a question of who has the strongest lungs or the most tireless pen. I shall, however, try to introduce some variations to break the monotony.

It is not difficult to meet Mr. Ingersoll's general arguments, his main, leading thought, but there is a subtle, crafty vein of sophism and implication running through them all which cannot be met by a reply to his main propositions. These shadowy, sinuous, winding, tortuous sophisms and implications, suggestive of the sardonic grin of a lurking Mephistopheles, must be met in some way. And the only possible way, it seems to me, is to separate his arguments into their component sentences, as the haymaker lifts sodden hay with his fork to let the sunlight and air purify, dry and shrivel it. His sentences thus separated and cleaned of their sophistry, we can look at them, see what they are worth, and value them accordingly.

This method I made use of on a former occasion in replying to Mr. Ingersoll's article on Judge Black. It is convenient, and, I believe, fair all around. I shall extenuate nothing or set nothing down in malice, but shall let Mr. Ingersoll speak for himself.

Now, Mr. Editor, after this short preface, I will introduce Mr. Ingersoll to your audience. Step forth, Colonel, and let us talk.

Ingersoll.— If he (De Costa) by Christianity means kindness, candor, the spirit of investigation, observation, reason,— in other words, if he aggregates what are called the virtues and calls them "Christianity,"— then there is no need to dispute.

Lambert.— Beg pardon; there will still be need for dispute or for better information. An aggregate of virtues does not and cannot constitute

Christianity or any other religion, any more than an aggregate of virtues constitutes a man, or an aggregate of different forces constitutes a locomotive, or an aggregate of brick, wood, and mortar constitutes a house. Virtue is a force or a facility of doing a thing with ease, arising from the doing of that thing many times, so many times as to acquire a habit of doing it. Kindness, candor, truthfulness, and the other moral virtues, are habits of mind growing out of frequent repetition of acts of kindness, candor, truthfulness. A truthful man is one who has acquired the habit of telling the truth and can do it without effort, so that even when speaking against Christianity he can tell it without danger of dislocating his jaw or bursting a blood vessel. We may then define virtue as a habit of mind inclining a man and making it easy for him to do good and act rightly. You can now see how these "habits of mind" may constitute a man good and religious, while they cannot constitute him a man, and why, taken altogether, they cannot constitute a religion or Christianity. Christianity teaches us all these virtues and exhorts us to practice them. That, together with the office of teaching revealed truth, is the mission of the Church of Christ, that Church which you are doing your best to discredit and dishonor. Virtue qualifies the man — it is a mode of his being. It is to him what the adjective is to the noun, and you need not be told that an aggregate of all the adjectives in language cannot constitute a noun. So you will see that the hypothetical case you put to Dr. De Costa is the pink and perfection of absurdity. You may now proceed.

Ingersoll.—Every religion teaches a code of morals plus something else.

Lambert.—Every religion first teaches truth, or what it believes to be truth, for without this as a basis or foundation no code of morals can exist. For instance, religion must first teach the existence of God before it can teach his will, law or revelation, as without the former the latter cannot be. From this first truth of philosophy, as well as of religion, arises the moral law; all morality, as the fruit of the tree, springs from its roots. Thus religion teaches us a fundamental principle, the existence of a Supreme Being, and that morality is founded on the relation between this Infinite Intelligence and finite intelligences, and that from this relation arises the duties, obligations, responsibilities and rights of man. These constitute the moral law or code. Without this Being there can be no moral code. I do not mean to say that those who deny the existence of this Being have no rule of conduct, but if they have a rule it is a borrowed one, a code not deduced from their own principles, but taken surreptitiously from that fundamental principle of Christianity, the existence of the Being Whom we call God, which they ostentatiously deny. To come back, you will observe that instead of every religion teaching a moral code plus something else, every religion begins with a fundamental truth, and then something else — the moral law. You simply change the idea.

Ingersoll.— Buddhism is a code of morals.

Lambert.— A moment ago you said: "Every religion *teaches* a code of morals." You now say the religion of Buddha *is* a code of morals. This confusion of utterance arises from a confusion of ideas. If your ideas are clear, you certainly have the ability to put them into clear English. A code of morals is no more a religion than the Declaration of Independence is the present administration, or the constitution of the United States, the government of the United States. Can you not get this distinction into your head? Buddhism is a religion which teaches certain doctrines on which it bases a certain code of morals. This distinction being evident, your whole argument based on your confusion of ideas, falls to the ground.

Ingersoll.— So Christianity is a code of morals plus —

Lambert.— Tut, tut, man; be reasonable. Don't repeat that blunder.

Ingersoll.— Plus that the God of the Old Testament is the Creator of the Universe.

Lambert.— Christianity teaches, first, a *truth* — the existence of the Supreme, Infinite, Eternal Being, on Whose existence, nature and relation to man it bases the Christian code of morals. You may call this Being the God of this, that, or the other, if you think it serves your purpose, but keep well in mind what Christianity teaches. The Being is the God of all that is, old or new, the Christian, the Jew and the pagan. But what you really meant to insinuate was this: The God of Christians is the same God Who, according to you, approved of all the murders, crimes and cruelties recorded in the Old Testament. According to your idea, this God is a monster. But you must pardon me if I decline to accept your account of Him or your "idea" of Him. I once reviewed your statements on this subject and showed that you misquoted, misrepresented and tortured out of their natural and obvious sense many texts of the Old Testament. I called that review, "Notes on Ingersoll." You made no reply to it. When Mr. Palmer, of the Nineteenth Century Club, proposed to you to discuss Christianity before that club, you expressed a willingness to do so, and asked who was to take the other side. He suggested my name and you declined, assigning as a reason that I was a Casuist. Mr. Palmer, I need not say, made that proposal to you without my knowledge or consent. If he had proposed to me an oral discussion with you I should have declined, for the reason that I have more faith in the virtue of cold type. I make the above statement on the authority of General George A. Sheridan. General Sheridan — unlike Moses and Judge Black — is not dead; and he has the advantage over them, that he can speak for himself.* Mentioning General Sheridan moves me to say that his lecture on "The Modern Pagan" is one of the best replies to Ingersollism that has been made. But to return —

---

*When I made the above statement, it occurred to me that "Slippery Bob" might be tempted to deny its truth as he denied some matters in relation to Judge Black — after his death. I therefore communicated with General Sheridan and received from him a letter from which I take the following extract: —

LONDON, ENGLAND, March 6, 1892.
23 BEDFORD PLACE, RUSSELL SQUARE, W. C.

MY DEAR FATHER: —

. . . As to the matter of your telegram, A. C. Wheeler was my first informant. Mr. Palmer afterwards confirmed his statement. My recollection is that the reason he gave for not meeting you was that you were "a mere Casuist."

Sincerely your friend,
GEO. A. SHERIDAN.

The Wheeler here referred to is the well-known art critic of the New York *World*. I am thus particular about this as it gives Ingersoll's shallow followers the rare opportunity of seeing how their Prophet looks with his mouth shut.

Ingersoll.—Christianity is a code of morals . . . plus certain ceremonies and superstitions.

Lambert.—We have already seen that neither Christianity nor any other religion is, or can be, a code of morals. Ceremonies are external signs or symbols indicative of the interior thought or belief, whether the belief be true or false. They symbolize what religion, true or false, believes to be true. Hence all ceremonies in the last analysis rest on truth, or what one believes to be truth. They are, therefore, plus to truth, not plus to a moral code, as you say. Be good enough to remember that a code of morals is not truth, but a sequence of truth. You may say these are small matters; but many of your conclusions are the result of an aggregate of small errors injected ignorantly or otherwise into your main line of argument, and it is my task just now to show that all your arguments against Christianity are thoroughly salted and peppered with just such small matters. That is what makes it so tiresome to reply to you, when one of your paragraphs, crammed with sophisms of speech and thought, requires a column to let light and air through it. So much for ceremonies, now for superstitions.

"Superstition" is one of the most useful words in the agnostic dictionary. It is hard to imagine how infidels could get on without it. It is such an excellent *argument*, so handy to throw in to fill a vacuum. It generally comes in as a tail to Ingersoll's list of Christian delinquencies. It is the cracker on the end of the whip to round off a sentence with a snap.

We have to say of superstition what we have said of ceremonies — that it cannot be plus to or predicated of a code of morals. Superstition, in all its multifarious forms, arises from a false belief or a false apprehension of true belief. Hence, its reference is to the true or the false, and not to the good or the bad. Now, Christianity teaches the truth. This proposition must stand until you disprove it, and do not forget that the *onus probandi* is on you.* As Christianity teaches the truth it affords

---

*As a correspondent in the *Evening Telegram* questioned the correctness of this statement, I will here show why I made it. It is a well-known maxim, as sound in logic as in jurisprudence, that possession is nine points of the law. Christianity is in possession — is the common belief in the civilized world. Our customs, habits of thought, laws, national and international, and the foundations of our governments rest on the teachings of Christianity. So, right or wrong, true or false, it is a fact that Christianity is in possession, and therefore he who would dispossess it must show cause why it should be dispossessed. It other words, the *onus probandi* is on him. When Christianity came into the world paganism was in possession, and as a consequence the *onus probandi* was on Christianity. It supplied the proof and in time took possession and has held it for cenno basis for superstition to rest on. The individual Christian apprehends correctly the truth as taught by Christianity or he does not. If he does he is not superstitious for he believes the truth as it is. If he does not apprehend the truth as taught by Christianity, he may fall into superstitious errors, but in that case his superstitions must be attributed to himself, not to Christianity which did not teach him his errors. The question then resolves itself into, whether Christianity teaches truth or not. By truth, I mean all truth of the moral order as contradistinguished from truths of the physical order. It won't do to say Christianity favors superstition and then pass on to argue as if the point were conceded. You must prove your statement and give us a bill of particulars. When

---

turies and holds it now. In face of this it is too late to demand title deeds. As a matter of fact, however, Christianity does supply these deeds. They are found in all theological and philosophical Christian literature.

But if Christianity does this it is not that it is, at this day, logically bound to do it. The question here is of logical obligation, whether the *onus* lies with the Christian or with him who would oust Christianity from possession. When a man makes an assertion CONTRARY to the common belief, it is his duty to give good reasons in its support. If he cannot, he should give up his assertion and go back to the common belief. Common beliefs, on the contrary, are in no need of special demonstration so long as they are not attacked by plausible reasons. Where Christianity is the common belief, the infidel has no logical right to demand the grounds

you do so, we will consider whether they are superstitions or not.

Webster defines superstition as "an excessive reverence or fear of that which is unknown or mysterious." Do you pretend that Christianity teaches, favors or winks at what is defined here? Excessive fear is the attribute of a coward; that cringing, slavish, craven fear which make a soldier slink from the ranks of his brave fellows and sneak under cover, or that fear which makes a cur throw himself on his back at the sight of a threatening cane. Christianity frowns on that fear which prevents a man from doing his duty, whether in the battle of brigades or the battle of life, and exalts moral courage as one of the noble attributes of man. But there is a fear that is noble and wise.

---

of that common belief. It is for him to show cause why that common belief should be abandoned. The *onus* is on him. Presumption is always in favor of possession, in logic as well as in law. Again, presumption is in favor of innocence till guilt is proved, and the first step to remove a supposed evil is to prove it is an evil. It is not for the supposed evil — so long as it is in possession — to prove that it is a good. The fact that it is in possession, necessitates the production of reasons why it should be removed. The *onus* is on him who would remove it. This is the logical situation in a discussion between the Christian and the infidel. It won't do for the infidel to shout out to the human race: "Prove the existence of God." The race has at all times and places believed in the existence of God, and it is the duty of the infidel to show cause why he makes himself an

It is that fear which the Scriptures tell us is the "beginning of wisdom." This is the fear of a brave man who dreads disgrace or fears death in an unworthy cause. The truly brave man is not he who fears no danger, but the man whose mind subdues the fear and braves the danger that nature shrinks from, when duty calls. Marlborough once said on going into action: "This poor body trembles at what the mind within is about to do." Fortitude and sense of duty should go hand in hand with fear and regulate it, not destroy it. The fear of God which Christianity inspires is in no way inconsistent with the dignity of man. It is a rational and proper fear inseparable from that august reverence which a finite intelligence experiences in the presence of the Infinite Intelligence,

---

exception to this common belief. If he gives good reasons they will be considered, but the world will not stop to give him a reason why it believes as it does. In all properly constituted canines the dog wags the tail. The advocates of Christianity are too apt to permit themselves to be thrown on the defensive and assume the *onus probandi*. When the infidel loudly informs the world that he does not believe there is a God, he should be asked for his reasons, and those reasons should be examined and refuted, but no attempt should be made to prove to him what the human race has always and everywhere believed. Keep him strictly to the logic of his position. Make him produce the proofs. Persist in this line of discussion and in a very short time he will be an exceedingly uninteresting passenger.
He who would change an existing order of things must

and on apprehending the relation in which it stands to Him. There is no superstition about this. Cringing, craven fear is not pleasing to the Supreme Being because it is an unworthy and false worship of Him, beneath the dignity of man, and is only found in those in whom brute nature predominates. The fear of hell is a rational fear, and is no more inconsistent with manliness in man than is the fear which inspires one to step from the track to avoid an advancing locomotive.

It is natural to man to avoid danger, and he should always do so unless duty requires him to brave it. While Christianity teaches a wholesome fear of eternal punishment, it does not offer it as the best motive of obedience to God, or of an honest and virtuous life. It teaches that love is the prime motive of human action, while fear is secondary and subsidiary. Our Lord said: "Thou shalt love the Lord thy God with thy whole heart,

---

assume the burden of showing why that order should be changed, just as he who would move a body at rest must bring to bear sufficient force to put that body in motion It is not for that body to give reasons why it should not be moved. In the laws of physics the fact that it is at rest is reason sufficient why it should remain so. Christianity is the order of the civilized world, and he who would change that order must assume the *onus probandi*. These are the reasons why I said, when the infidel attacks Christianity the *onus probandi* is on him.

with thy whole soul, and with thy whole strength, and thy neighbor as thyself." And St. Paul says: "All the law is fulfilled in one sentence. Love thy neighbor as thyself." Texts of this intention are scattered all through the Scriptures, but your intellectual strabismus will not permit you to see them. This is the love which Christianity inculcates as the first, truest and noblest motive to avoid evil and do good. And the fear which the same religion presents to us as a motive to do good and avoid evil, is that fear which the child has of the father it loves, the fear to offend, the fear to lose his love and break that golden chain that binds their hearts in mutual affection. But enough of this at present. I have made this digression, suggested by Webster's definition of superstition, because you are constantly representing Christianity as inculcating a slavish, cringing, craven fear, and that Our Father Who is in heaven smiles on this base, degrading abjection as Moloch smiles on flowing blood and quivering flesh.

Ingersoll.— No one objects to the morality of Christianity.

Lambert.— There is a suspicious frankness about this, and the reader may bet a nickle with himself that there is a hook to it. It is always well to suspect excessively pious pretensions and excessive frankness, for a hypocrite may lurk under either. It is the very frankness of the confidence man that disarms his victims.

Ingersoll.— The industrious people of the world— those who have anything — are, as a rule, opposed to larceny.

Lambert.— I knew it ; and now, reader, you may put your nickel in your other vest pocket. It is not Christian morals that larceny is wrong because people object to it, and in insinuating the idea you misrepresent Christian theology. It is wrong because God Almighty objects, and He objects because it is antagonistic to His own eternal justice. This is the Christian idea, and you will observe it is very different from your idea, which is absurd, for if the wrong of larceny consisted in people's objecting it would be equally wrong to collect debts, for most people object to it; equally wrong to collect taxes for the same reason. So you will see that the sense in which you agree with Christian morality is not the sense in which Christianity enforces it. When you thought you were agreeing you were not, and in this you possibly deceived even yourself. Will you please give your idea of right and wrong, and tell us the ultimate principle on which you base the distinction between them;

in other words, what is your standard of right and wrong?

Ingersoll.— Consequences determine the quality of actions. If consequences are good, so is the action.

Lambert.— Then the question whether larency is a good or a bad act must remain unanswered until the consequences of the act are definitely known. The man whose pocketbook was stolen must be cheerful and patient and wait for the consequences before he can know whether he has been wronged or not, or whether after all the thief did not do a good act. The loss of the money has lost him his farm and sent him and his wife and little ones barefooted and hungry into the highway to face the pitiless blasts of winter, and made the babe cry in vain for the breast that hunger had made powerless to nourish it. Surely suffering has come as a consequence of the act — but not to the thief, whose experience we will see later on. In this state of awful desolation the poor farmer meets Mr. Ingersoll and says : " Oh, sir, see the horror of my situation! Do you think that thief did wrong to bring upon me this suffering? See my wife, her eyes are dull and stupid from cold and hunger, sir! See that babe, how it clings to the sapless breast! God help it, it is more fortunate than its father; it suffers without consciousness of suffering and will die without knowing that it ever lived in this world. Thanks be to the good God, it has not my consciousness to take in all this horror that God never intended me or mine to suffer! But see, it is dying — it is dead, dead, and the stupid mother knows it not. Oh, Mr. Ingersoll, did not that man do me a woeful wrong?" To this appeal you would reply, if you are true to your principles: "I do not know if he did wrong or not; I must wait to see the consequences of his act, I must wait and see how his act affects *him*. If he has done wrong Nature will punish him, but I cannot know whether he did wrong or not till I know the consequences of his act. Yours is only one side of the case. I must see *his* family, and his children's children's children and so on indefinitely or infinitely before I can give an honest opinion about it." The wife dies, the children go to the poorhouse, and the father to the madhouse, and thus ends that side. Now for the thief.

Court opens. Policeman produces prisoner, who admits fact, but claims he did not do wrong. Judge (Ingersollian) announces that prisoner's plea bars Court from further action, till all the consequences of his act are known, since on these depend his innocence or guilt. Prisoner released for want of evidence; must await evidence — the consequences of his act, all of which are not yet known. Ingersoll offers to testify to consequences he has seen. His evidence taken and recorded. Court adjourns for further evidence — consequences not all in yet. How long must they wait? Now, Mr. Ingersoll, as you are strong on the sciences, you know that not a particle of matter, in any part of the material universe, can be moved without affecting every other particle of matter in the same universe; that when you toss the ashes from your cigar you change the course of the moon, the sun and all the planets and suns, visible and invisible, that move in silence through space; and that the perturbation you produce will prevent all these from ever being again as they were before. Can you or anybody calculate and sum up the physical consequences of your act, the net result, in all the countless æons of time to come? It may seem strange that the fall of a bit of ashes or the movement of a fly's wing can produce such an endless commotion, but science, you know, leaves no doubt of it. Just here, Mr. Ingersoll, I must ask you if the goodness or badness of the thief's act is to be known by its physical or moral consequences. If you say by the physical, I reply that from the scientific facts I have just given, it is absolutely impossible to know, in time or eternity, whether the thief did a good or a bad thing. And a code of morals that leaves things in that condition is not fit for a lunatic asylum.

If you say the goodness or badness of the thief's act depends on moral consequences, I reply that, judging by analogy from what we know by experience and science, we must conclude that the moral world is governed by the same laws that govern the physical world. And if you grant this, which, as a scientist, you know is perfectly scientific, we will have to go through the same endless round as in the case of the ashes and fly's wing. But you may deny this analogy. Well, then, I will let it pass and take your own theory, that all there is is matter, and that all phenomena known to us, whether moral, intellectual or physical, are nothing but forms of matter. From this dogma of yours it evidently follows that the physical, moral, intellectual worlds are governed by the same law. Then what I have said of the endless consequences of a physical act is equally true of a moral act. Let us now see the consequences of the thief's act in the moral world, and try if we can ever know them. The act of the thief from the moment of its doing will begin and continue to work out its consequences,—by which its goodness or badness is to be known,—and the moral world will never be the same as it was before the thieving act. The moral wave, put in motion by the thief, will roll on forever, now meeting opposing billows, now swerving at an unknowable angle, and, baffled, turning its course elsewhere, but never again to find that equilibrium and rest in which the thief found it before his act. Now, if your theory of right and wrong be true, it can never be known in the moral world whether the thief did a good thing or a bad, till the moral consequences of his acts are summed up and the net result known. This summing up becomes the more difficult if we count in the consequences, physical and moral, to the poor farmer, and what remains of his wrecked family. But what of the court and the thief? Why, the court may adjourn to eternity and the plaintiff and the jury be damned, and yet the plain question: Did the thief do wrong? must remain forever unanswered.

In this age of reason and common sense is it really necessary to refute such a standard of judgment in morals? A standard, to be of any value whatever, must enable a man to tell the nature of an act when he is required or tempted to do it — before he does it, that he may do it if good or refrain from doing it if bad. To know this afterwards is too late to be of any benefit to him. And life is too short to await the consequences. We have seen the end of the poor farmer and his family. We will now see how the thief got on after his act. The Court reopens. The thief is there, hale, hearty, fat and chipper. Ingersollian Judge on the bench:—

Court.— Mr. Prisoner, you are accused of having done wrong. You are an intelligent-looking man; in fact, you are a sharp-looking man. You look like a man who can take care of himself and get on in this villainous world. You have the appearance of a prosperous man. You are fat, which shows that your fellow-citizens have implicit confidence in you, else they would not have elected you an Alderman. You look happy and contented, which shows that within your ample being there dwells a peaceful, loving, agnostic kind of a spirit — if you happen to have any. But under present circumstances I feel for you. You stand in the prisoner's box humiliated. I would feel rather badly if I were in your place, and I am glad I am not. But, being like yourself an agnostic, I don't know for certain. I feel for you,— at least I think I do,— but I may be wrong. I never traveled in any other world but this, and I am, in consequence, provincial. I cannot see clearly how a just and powerful government, which you could not hurt, even if you tried ever so hard, can have the heart to put you to any inconvenience. But this is a bloodthirsty Christian government, and we've got to keep our eyes open wide or they will persecute us. Do you take in the idea? They will *persecute* us; yes, *persecute*. They spell it *prosecute*, not knowing better. They will stop at nothing, these bloody-handed minions of priestcraft and superstition. It is a happy circumstance that you are not a scientist, for they have a hankering after raw scientist. You are an artist, however, and that is why you are here. If you know anything don't let them remark it, or burned brandy and brimstone won't save you. Speaking of brandy reminds me that time is passing, and without further remarks, Mr. Prisoner, we will pass on to business. You are charged with doing wrong, what is your plea?

Thief.— Your Honor, the police, those tools of a steel-hearted tyranny, inspired by the fiendish, diabolical and blood-guzzling genius of Christianity, with hands reeking with the blood of scientists, brought me here, and charge me with having done wrong — yes, wrong, your Honor. (Here prisoner gives way to his feelings and the Judge shows emotion.)

Court.— What did you do?

Thief.— I stole $5,000, your Honor.

Court.— And what were the consequences?

Thief.— With the money I bought a house, a new suit of clothes all round for my wife and little ones, and some candy for the baby. Your Honor's heart would have melted if you had seen how that baby's eyes danced and how his little chubby legs kicked when he saw it. He's an agnostic baby, your Honor.

Court.— May the court, without offense, ask why you think so; that is, you don't object?

Thief.— No objection in the world, your Honor. The little tootsy-wootsy actually put it in his mouth without missing. A Christian baby sticks it in his ear.

Court.— Or eye — practicing to stick redhot iron into other people's eyes and ears,— shows the instinct early. Persecution in the blood. But, prisoner, did you get all this happiness out of your theft?

Thief.— Yes, your Honor, these were the happy consequences of my little operation.

Court.— Gentlemen of the jury, this case is so clear and pellucid that I do not think it necessary to impose on your powerful minds the burden of giving a verdict. The prisoner frankly admits that he stole. This frankness is to be highly commended, being so seldom found, except among agnostics. If there is anything under the ethereal blue that this Court admires more than another, it is candor and courage of the soul. These qualities are not always found in thieves, I am sorry to say.

This thief, then, is, to quote the words of the immortal Latin bard, whose name I forget, and you, gentlemen of the jury, probably never knew, a *rara avis in terris*. He admits he committed the theft charged, but claims that it was the result of free thought, and that in realizing his free thought he was under the necessity of making free with farmer Jones' pocketbook. He claims that the theft had the happiest consequences, and that therefore it was a good act. In doing it he had an eye single and honest to the happiness of his family. He has pictured before you a scene of domestic felicity as the result of his theft which, stealing on the imagination, leads us to believe that all virtue is not extinct. He has painted before our mind's eye, with all the skill of a Raphael or an Angelo,— who were great in spite of their Christianity,— a picture of his happy family circle living on the money of Mr. Jones. Nothing but the happiest consequences have followed from the action of this candid thief. Prisoner, you can go; your act was good and praiseworthy, as Mr. Ingersoll will tell you, on account of its consequences. The officer who arrested you will pay the costs, and make an apology or take the consequences.

Lambert.— Your standard of morality, Mr. Ingersoll, may suit the agnostic, but it does not commend itself to a plain, common-sense Christian people.

Ingersoll.— A large majority of people object to being murdered.

Lambert.— But their objection does not constitute the malice of murder. Murder would be equally wrong even if the victim consented. You are inconsistent in saying a murder is bad, until you know all the consequences of it, for in these, you tell us, its nature or quality is to be sought. The malice of murder, according to Christian teaching, consists in the fact that it is an outrage on the universe and its Creator, a war against universal order and harmony, a clash with the divine will. The murderer maliciously destroys a most perfect work of the Supreme Artist.

Ingersoll.— There is no very great difference of opinion among civilized people as to what is or is not moral.

Lambert.— One reason of that is, that most civilized people pay no attention to your philosophy or to your moral standard. The great majority of civilized people are Christians, they have the Ten Commandments, and that is the reason why they do not differ as to what is or is not moral.

Ingersoll.— It cannot be truthfully said that the man who attacks Buddhism attacks all morality.

Lambert.— You attack a religion when you attack its doctrines. If you attack the doctrines or dogmas of Buddhism you attack the moral code based on those doctrines.

Ingersoll.— So, one attacking what is called Christianity does not attack kindness, charity, or any other virtue.

Lambert.— You attack these virtues when you destroy the motives of them. You attack them when you destroy the reason of their being. When you deny God and hold the doctrine of unavoidable fate, you take away all the motives of virtuous acts. Since, if they are *necessary* acts, they cease to be virtues. The virtues cannot exist where there is no free will, where our thoughts grow out of what we eat, as you teach. Christianity teaches us the existence of a Supreme Being Who holds us responsible for our acts, and rewards or punishes us for them. Hence, when you attack these fundamental truths of Christianity, you destroy those virtues, as you would destroy a house by removing its foundation, or as you would kill the branches by cutting down the tree. The virtues are the bloom and fruit of truth worked out in human action.

Ingersoll.— He attacks something that has been added to the virtues.

Lambert.— This begs the question. Before attacking this "something that has been added to the virtues" you should show what it is — give a bill of particulars, that we may see about them. If Christianity teaches the truths, from which all the virtues flow as a result, it should receive the credit.

Ingersoll.— There were millions of virtuous men and women before Christianity was known.

Lambert.— No doubt of it. But the foundation of their virtues was the belief in the existence of the Supreme Being, and obedience to His law written on the heart of every man that comes into this world. That same law and the existence of that same Being are what Christianity teaches. The Commandments were only *reiterated* on Mount Sinai. It is very certain that those millions of virtuous men and women you speak of were not made so by agnostic philosophy.

Ingersoll.— It does not seem possible to me that love, kindness, justice or charity ever caused any one who possessed and practiced these virtues to persecute his fellowman on account of a difference of belief.

Lambert.— Christianity inculcates kindness, charity, truthfulness, justice, etc. If a Christian fails to practice these virtues, the fault is his own and cannot be attributed to the religion whose teachings he disregards. You harp much on persecutions for difference of *belief*. I do not believe that any persecution ever took place for a mere difference of belief. There was always difference of belief plus something else. It is a fact of human nature that no man can attempt to overthrow the fixed maxims and beliefs of any people without getting himself into trouble. Belief produces in man corresponding external acts. By these external acts a man may come in collision with somebody else or with the laws of society. Then comes the trouble. As long as the Southern people believed in the right of secession, no one interfered with them. When that belief took the shape of muskets and artillery, the Government crushed it out. It would not be true to say that war was made on them on account of a difference of belief. The Mormons believe in polygamy. As long as they did not practice the belief, they were let alone. When they put it into practice, Congress legislated against it and punished the guilty. They say they are persecuted for their belief, but you know it is not true. We can understand how good, kind and just men will oppose and persecute them if they disregard the law. Our Government does not legislate against Anarchists but when some Anarchists put their belief into practice in Chicago they were hanged. They call it persecution. Apply these suggestions to the history of the past and you will find that difference in belief, was not the cause of persecutions, but belief plus something else which was opposed to the maxims and customs of the people. Connected with belief there were practices which offended society and aroused opposition and bloodshed. Hence, all the talk of persecution for difference of belief is mere cant.

Ingersoll.— If Christianity has persecuted, some reason must exist outside the virtues inculcated.

Lambert.— As Christianity did not persecute, it is needless to seek reasons why she did. Whether some Christian peoples persecuted is another question. And I deny that Christian peoples persecuted for difference of belief alone. I have given the reason above. The cause of persecution must be sought outside of the truths and principles inculcated by Christianity.

Ingersoll.— If this cause is inherent in something

else, which has been added to the ordinary virtues, then Christianity can properly be held accountable for the persecution.

Lambert.— *Nego suppositum.* Unless Christianity added this mysterious " something else " to the ordinary virtues, it cannot properly be held accountable for persecutions. It is denied that Christianity added this, which you slyly assume.

Ingersoll.— Of course, back of Christianity is the nature of man, and, primarily, it may be responsible.

Lambert.— Here I think you have struck bottom. Human nature, as found concreted in the individual man, has both good and bad impulses, appetites and emotions. One moment he drops the tear of pity on the brow of pain, the next moment, maddened by passion, he plunges the knife into the heart of his victim. His blood is feverish and restless, his darkened mind caters to a weakened will and always finds some pretense to justify him when he strikes the cruel blow. Sometimes he will pretend that his act is inspired by zeal for religion ; at other times, love of liberty nerved his blood-seeking hand. An excuse never fails him. Sometimes he seeks cover under candor, honor bright, courage of the soul, etc., etc. He steals the livery of all these to cover his real motive, but when he ascribes his evil deeds to any or all these, he is a hypocrite. It is a case of *non causa pro causa*. Christianity endeavors to instruct this bundle of impulses called man, to supply him with principles and motives of action, to regulate his actions; in a word to educate, soften, refine and civilize him. But it is hard to do, and false teachers and false philosophers make it still more difficult.

Ingersoll.— Is there anything in Christianity to account for such persecutions — the Inquisition?

Lambert.— No, there is not. We have found in fallen human nature the cause of it, and need seek no further.

But the Inquisition? He who studies the history of Spain in the fifteenth century will be convinced that the Court of the Inquisition was a proper and necessary measure to prevent the destruction of the Spanish nation. Every government has the right to take the necessary measures to defend its existence. No one, not even revolutionists, will deny this political maxim. During our late war President Lincoln proclaimed several States under martial law. The sympathizers with the revolt made a howl about it and shouted tyranny, despotism. But no one now thinks of doubting the justice and necessity of the great President's act in proclaiming martial law. The ordinary courts and processes are for times of peace. They were not quick and thorough enough to meet the case and deal promptly and swiftly with treason and conspiracy. But treason and conspiracy must be met when the life of a nation is in peril. At a time when the existence of Spain was in peril, Ferdinand and Isabella established the Court of the Inquisition, or Court of Inquiry, to meet and overcome the political evils of the times. It is a political axiom that no sensible man ever denied that *great political evils, and especially violent acts leveled at the body of the State, can never be repelled except by measures equally violent.* The rule of ancient Rome is the standard by which danger to the state must be measured and met. *Videant consules ne respublica detrimentum capiat. Let the consuls see that the government sustain no injury.* The most successful means to meet and crush revolution is invariably the best. These measures may differ at different times, owing to circumstances and degrees of civilization, but the rule always stands good.

But it was in the name of religion, you say. Religion, through circumstances, was made the war cry, just as liberty is made the war cry, or the rose the war cry between the houses of York and Lancaster. It matters little what the shibboleth may be, when men, white with passion, clinch.

But they punished heretics! When heresy became a synonym of treason, conspiracy and rebellion, it was punished as such. The Spanish state struck the traitor, conspirator and revolutionist wherever it found him, heretic or not. History shows that treason and heresy were intimately allied at the time. But why not strike the heretic who is a traitor to the state? Should his heresy be a shield for his treason? There is a great deal of maudlin sentiment wasted on the victims of the Inquisition. The Inquisition was a political institution — a court martial — established to meet a great danger to the state, and it ceased to exist when the danger ceased.

But the cruelties of it? That cruelties were committed there is no doubt, but abuse is inseparable from the exercise of absolute power in the hands of men. But if we must condemn the court for the cruelties of a Torquemada, we must also condemn the whole fabric of English jurisprudence for the cruelties of a Jeffreys or a Norbury.

Ingersoll.— It certainly was taught by the Church that belief was necessary to salvation.

Lambert. — And is still so taught.

Ingersoll.— And it was thought at the same time that the fate of man was eternal punishment.

Lambert.— This statement is not true. And even

if it were so thought, Christianity is not responsible, as it taught no such doctrine.

Ingersoll.— It was taught that the state of man was that of depravity, and that there was but one way by which he could be saved, and that was through faith.

Lambert.— The Church taught that man was saved by faith and good works, which are the flower and fruit of faith. Salvation is the reward of these two, going hand in hand.

Ingersoll.— As long as this was honestly believed —

Lambert.— As if one could *dishonestly* believe!

Ingersoll.— Christians would not allow heretics or infidels to preach a doctrine to their wives, to their children, or to themselves, which, in their judgment, would result in the damnation of their souls.

Lambert.— And why should they allow it? Do you believe that any "honestly" conscientious Christian would allow you or a Mormon elder to preach your "notions" to his wife and children? But to prevent you or the elder, it is not necessary to kill you. One could call a policeman to abate the nuisance.

Ingersoll.— The law gives a man the right to kill one who is about to do great bodily harm to his son.

Lambert.— I am not aware that even civil law gives such a right, and I know that the divine law does not.* Christianity teaches no such doctrine.

Ingersoll.— Now if the father has the right to take the life of a man simply because he is attacking the body of his son —

Lambert.— But he has not the right.

Ingersoll.— How much more would he have the right to take the life of one who is about to assassinate the soul of his son.

Lambert.— This conclusion is based on a false hypothesis, on false premises, and is therefore worthless. It is, however, a very good specimen of Ingersollian logic.

---

*A writer in the *Freethinker's Magazine* who, the editor tells us, is "a leading lawyer of Chicago," after quoting my words in the text, comments as follows:—

"If you are not aware that the civil law gives such a right, Colonel Ingersoll will gladly lend you his text-book and you can find it out for yourself. You will find it stated there so plainly that it will be impossible for you to misunderstand it or deny it."

On reading this I consulted several lawyers — among them a district attorney and a justice of the supreme court of New York. The lawyers, without a dissenting voice, said that the proposition, as stated by Ingersoll, is not the law. The district attorney said: "Ingersoll's proposition is too broad. It is not the law. As a general proposition with no conditions stated, it would be more nearly accurate to say: 'A father has not the right to kill a man who is about to do serious bodily harm to his son.'" The supreme judge said: "A man may use just so much force in defending him-

I.S.C.—5

Ingersoll.— Christians reason in this way.

Lambert.— No, they don't. They repudiate any such argument for the reason that it is neither true nor logical. In Christian ethics a man can and should defend his child from harm, and if in this defense his own life is in such peril that he or the unjust aggressor must die, he can kill him, not otherwise. But even if your hypothesis were true, your conclusions would not follow, because it introduces a term that is not in the premises. There is no analogy between killing the body and killing the soul in the same sense. No man can *hic et nunc* kill the soul. He may place a cause, say false teaching or bad example, which may ultimately lead to the damnation of the soul, but he cannot place a cause that leads directly and necessarily to

---

self or another as is necessary, or justly seems to him necessary, to prevent the threatened injury and no more."

While these lawyers agreed that Ingersoll was wrong, they were so far influenced by what Bacon calls the "idol of the tribe" as to say they believed that Ingersoll meant all right but failed to state what he meant fully enough.

A distinguished lawyer of the Colorado bar said:—

"1. The law is that a father may slay one who attempts the life of his son, if the criminal assault is made in such a way as to create a just apprehension of imminent danger of death, or great bodily harm to the child.

"2. Past threats or conduct of the person killed, however violent, will not excuse homicide; no contingent necessity will avail the slayer. There must be overt acts indicative of immediate danger at the time of killing the assailant.

"3. Argument that the aggressor was attacking the son

that end. But he can place a cause that leads necessarily and directly to the death of the body, say, cutting off the head or plunging a dagger through the heart. In this case the account must be settled then and there. But you cannot kill a man to-day to avoid a death he may inflict on you forty years hence. To conclude, first, your premises are false; second, your conclusion does not follow from your premises, even if they were granted.

Ingersoll.— In addition they felt that God would hold them responsible if the community allowed the blasphemer to attack the true religion.

Lambert.— However they may have felt, they did right to legislate against blashemy and jail the foul-mouthed blasphemer till he learned decency and better manners. If he attacks the fixed max-

---
must show, in addition, clearly the immediate danger, then and there, at once, of death or great bodily harm which could only be warded off by killing the assailant.

"4. If a father, in the necessary defense of his child as stated, is himself in immediate danger of death at the hands of the aggressor, or of great bodily harm, he certainly may slay such aggressor.

"5. 'These are the doctrines of Universal Justice as well as of the Municipal Law,' said Lord Blackstone. 4th Bk., Com. 185.

"From the established principles here laid down, it is evident that Ingersoll has not, in the words quoted from him, correctly stated the law."

These views correspond perfectly with the principles of theology, the dictates of reason and the natural moral law.

In other words, Colonel Ingersoll failed to state the law.

ims and prevailing belief of a people he must not plead the "baby act" after having aroused them to rid themselves of what they consider a public nuisance.

Ingersoll.— And therefore they killed the freethinker, or rather, the free talker, in self-defense.

Lambert.— As we have seen that your premises are false, the conclusion is false. Hence, if they killed the freethinkers, it was not *therefore*, but for something else. It appears that it was not the freethinker who was killed for his "think," but the free talker for his talk. Many men have been killed for their talk, and many will be as long as man has passions. When free talk causes disturbance and disorder and threatens the peace and prosperity of society or the security of the state, men — in all times and of all religions — have been in the habit of silencing the disturber in one way or another, and they will continue to do so, and call it prosecution — not persecution.

Ingersoll.— If the founder of Christianity had said —

Is he as untrustworthy in his own chosen profession as in his comments on Moses? He seems to have an innate obliqueness of mental vision that makes it almost impossible for him to present a fact or a law or a truth correctly. It has been the general impression that Chicago had some able lawyers. If George Norton Benedict is a leading one among them, he has a strange way of showing it.

Lambert.— We will speak of that in our next conversation. This vast audience, procured to us by the love of fair play and enterprise of the *Telegram*, have had enough for the present. They have been severely tried of late.

CHAPTER II.

Ingersoll.— If the founder of Christianity had said: "It is not necessary to believe in order to be saved," . . . there would probably have been but little persecution.

Lambert.— What an improvement there would have been if you had been there to make suggestions. But it would have been still better if you had been a little earlier, that you could have given the Creater the benefit of your "idea." That August Being, the perfect wisdom and perfect manhood, before whom the greatest minds of the world have bowed in adoration, would have had some suggestions to make to you. He could be severe when the occasion required it. Though His eyes were dim with sorrow, His rebuking glance would have shrivelled the irreverent jest in your throat. He Who had words of compassion for the Magdalen and the thief, lashed with the whip of scorn the

Pharisee and the hypocrite. On the whole, perhaps it is better you were not there. Perhaps it never occurred to your mind that the reason He did not say what you think He ought to have said was that it is not true.

Ingersoll.— If He had added: "You must not persecute in My name. My religion is the religion of Love — not the religion of Force and Hatred. You must not imprison your fellowmen. You must not stretch them on racks or crush their bones in iron boots. You must not flay them alive. You must not cut off their eyelids nor pour melted lead into their ears," etc. . . . His followers would not have murdered their fellows in His name.

Lambert.— Your catalogue of new commandments is very incomplete. There are many ways of giving pain left out. Did your imagination lag or your pen tire? Why not have gone on? "You must not bore a hole in his tongue or in any member of his body or in muscle or sinew, etc. (for which see works on physiology). You must not burn holes in same or punch them. You must not cut same in same. You must not stick pins made of iron, steel or brass or aluminum into him. You must not stick needles into him, or into his feet or hands or fingers or toes. You must not put his head under a pump and pump on him. You must not exchange him for a mule, as a certain Southern general proposed to do with a certain Northern colonel." Thus you see you failed to get in all the agonies. You ought to give some suggestions to the author of the book on "Dont's." The founder of Christianity did not legislate in this retail way. He laid down a general principle which covers the whole ground. He said: "*Do unto others as you would that others should do unto you,*" and "*Love thy neighbor as thyself.*" How does this compare with your picayune formula? If men forget this sublime command, they are not followers of Christ.

Ingersoll.—If Christ was in fact God, He knew the persecutions that would be carried on in His name. He knew of the millions that would suffer death through torture. *Yet He died without saying one word to prevent what He must have known, if He were God, would happen.*

Lambert.—The statement italicized by me raises a question of fact. When you made it you were either ignorant of the teachings of Christ, or you made it with intent to deceive. There is no middle ground. You can choose either horn of the dilemma, but from one or the other you cannot escape. We will now see if Christ died *without saying one word* to prevent the death of millions:

"And Jesus said: 'Thou shalt do no murder.'" (Math. xix., 18.) Is not this enough to convict you of misrepresentation, wilful or otherwise? It is remarkable that Christ in this same verse, adds: "Thou shalt not bear false witness." Again, he continues in the next verse: "Thou shalt love thy neighbor as thyself." And in Luke vi., 31: "As you would that men should do unto you, do ye also to them likewise." Again: "Judge not and ye shall not be judged; condemn not and ye shall not be condemned; forgive and ye shall be forgiven." "If ye forgive men their trespasses, your heavenly Father will also forgive you; but if ye forgive not men their trespasses, neither will your Father forgive you your trespasses." (Math. vi., 14, 15.) I might quote other texts to the same effect, but enough has been given to prove that you are guilty of a historical untruth—you, who talk of candor and honor bright! It is certain that whatever code of morals you may follow, it is not the Christian code.

Ingersoll.—All that Christianity has added to morality is worthless and useless.

Lambert.—Without the truths taught by Christianity, there is and can be no morality. Take away the origin of moral obligation, and morality is removed with it. Take away the foundation and the superstructure falls. Remove the roots and the branches wither, and both blossom and fruit fall. Remove the fountain and the brook is dry. Hence, morality without God and His religion is zero — nothing. In supposing the existence of morality without God, you are guilty of a pitiful begging of the whole question. Your theory of eternal fate leaves man no motive to do right but fear of the chain-gang, the jail or the gibbet. Talk not, then, to the Christian about morality, when your principles make the very idea of it impossible. You who teach that man is a mere machine, whose thoughts and acts are the result of what he eats and digests, and that all he is or does is only a link in the endless chain of fate, can have no meaning, no thought corresponding to the word " Morality," and you should remove it from your terminology. There can be no moral code for that which acts from absolute and fatal necessity. He who would apply the word moral or immoral to a locomotive or a type-writing machine would be considered an incurable crank. The same is to be said of brute animals, who are controlled not by free will but by instinct. Morality is an attribute of a moral agent, and can have no existence where moral free agency is destroyed by the doctrine of fatal necessity. But notwithstanding this, and while you make man a mere machine grinding out ideas from whatever may be thrown into his hopper, you talk of morality and of what Christianity would be without it, and what it would be without Christianity, and such like meaningless verbiage.

Ingersoll.—Take Christianity away from morality and the useful is left.

Lambert.—Take away the truths taught by Christianity and you have no mortality left, because the reason of its being is taken away.

Ingersoll.—Take morality from Christianity and the useless is left.

Lambert.—When you take the foundation from the building it falls a shapeless mass of ruins. Christian truth is the foundation of morality.

Ingersoll.—Now, falling back on the old assertion: "By its fruits we may know Christianity," then, I think, we are justified in saying that, as Christianity consists of a mixture of morality and something else, and as morality never has persecuted a human being, and as Christianity has persecuted millions, the cause of persecution must be something else."

Lambert.—The sophistry of this piece of agnostic reasoning may be shown in several ways. Let us take a parallel illustration and see where it leads. It is a fact that thousands of men have been murdered in the United States from its beginning down to the Latimer, Pa., "incident." The question now is, who committed all this murder, where shall the responsibility be placed? Taking a leaf from Ingersollian logic, we proceed in this manner: The United States Government is a mixture of Constitution, a code of laws and something else. Now, as the Constitution and legislation did not murder these victims, it must have been something else that did it. This something else is the Government. Therefore, the Government of the United States committed all the murders that have been committed since its establishment. Of course, every admirer of our Government will be shocked at this agnostic conclusion and give the lie. We must agree with the indignant patriot and say: Yes, the conclusion is false, the argument is Ingersollian. Let us then proceed with the analysis till we find the murderers, for find them we must, or the Government is in for it. As these murders were not committed by the Constitution or code of laws or the Government, they were committed by something else. This something else can be only men and women.

We have now got down to the last element of the analysis, and must conclude that men and women committed the murders. I have left babies and sucklings out of the calculation, through respect for Mr. Ingersoll's nerves. Let us now go back to the question under consideration and see how this analysis works. As Christianity did not persecute (notwithstanding Mr. Ingersoll's assertion to the contrary), it must have been done by something else, and as there is no other imaginable agent in the bloody business, we must saddle it on men and women, babies excepted for the reason stated. And as men and women generally do evil things through evil motives and passions, we conclude that they persecuted their fellowmen and women to realize their evil motives and gratify their evil passions; and in doing so, to shield themselves, stole the livery of heaven to serve the devil in. Since the earth first drank human blood, spilled by Cain, it has thirsted for it, and men's passions slake the thirst, despite the voice that thundered from Sinai, and was repeated by the Son of Man: "Thou shalt do no murder." Christianity re-echoes this divine command through the ages, and still the incarnadined Niagara flows on.

Surely there must be a cause for all this desolation and mourning. Some awful crime must have been committed somewhere — some time. In this Rama of lamentation stands the Christian Church, a weeping Rachel, pointing, with shuddering hand, to Eden and the Man.

Ingersoll.—Human nature has been derided, has been held up to contempt and scorn, all our desires and passions denounced as wicked and filthy.

Lambert.— 1. *Human nature has been derided.* Yes, a late school of philosophy tells us we are all monkeys of a higher development, and talks of a lost caudal extremity, and how the habit of sitting around stunted the vertebral process. This is rather derisive, it must be confessed, but it is agnostic derision. You make man a machine. 2. *Hold up to contempt and scorn all our desires.* No; only evil, impure and filthy desires. 3. *And passions.* No; Christianity teaches that all our passions are good in themselves, because God-given. It is the abuse of them, or the improper control of them, that is condemned. They are to reason what a good horse is to the driver, or what steam is to the engineer. When trained and controlled good work can be got out of them, but when left to their own wild and vagrant impulses, they are apt to smash the vehicle or burst the boiler. Christianity exhorts us to govern the passions with a tight rein and a firm hand, and not let them get the bit in their teeth. So here, again, you run off with only a piece of an idea, thinking you had the whole of it.

Now, Mr. Ingersoll, as you have said so much about moral codes plus something else, and Christianity taken away from morality, etc., will you be good enough to give your idea of morality, or the standard of morals by which we may know whether an act is good or bad?

Ingersoll.— A man is a machine into which we put what we call food and produce what we call thought. Think of that wonderful chemistry, by which bread was changed into the divine tragedy of Hamlet. ("The Gods," page 47.)

Lambert.— In compliance with your suggestion, I have thought a good deal about it and have come to some interesting results, although you omitted to tell us what kind of food we should take in order to get the machine to think on the particular subject you suggest, or what you eat that made you suggest it. I must have struck the right diet, however, for I thought on what you suggested without the least difficulty, and it has thrown considerable light on my mind. Your idea is like the headlight of a locomotive to me. It bores a hole of light into dense darkness and reveals things before unseen. You make thought the chemical result of digested food. Then the nature and quality of thought depends on the nature and quality of food plus something else, viz., the condition and action of the stomach, kidneys, liver, bile duct, pylorus, duodenum, plus the peristaltic action, etc. Bread, it appears, comes out of this human alembic in the form of divine tragedy. It was just at this point the light struck me and I exclaimed, with the old Greek philosopher: "Eureka"—I have found it. Now, thought I, if I could only know Mr. Ingersoll's diet I would find the key to his whole system of philosophy. Not having his regular bill of fare at hand, I set to work to think out about what kind of victuals would produce certain well-known results, and Mr. Ingersoll may correct me if I am wrong. Thus, to think: For the "Mistakes of Moses," he loaded his hopper with desert quail of Arabia, Egyptian leeks and sacrificial mutton—to the dulcet strains of the Jews' harp. For "The Gods," he partook of a Barmecide feast, with honey of Hymettus and wine of Olymphus or Mytilene, served by Hebe or Ganymede. For the "Ghosts," welsh rarebit, mince pie, shrapnel, and other indigestible junk. For the "Christmas Sermon," the Christmas dinner, which must have been assimilated very quickly. If he replies to me, I ask it as a favor that he abstain for a time from mustard, pepper sauce and chicken, as I am not partial to hot shot or foul play.

Hereafter, when the Napoleon of Infidelity gets up a new lecture, his previous bill of fare will be a matter of public interest, and when he steps smilingly on the stage, his portly figure will suggest the question: Wonder what he's been eating this time? It is not surprising that he and I should differ so widely in philosophy, since he lives on the fat of the land and I on the lean — and fish. But why lose his time reasoning with human alembics? Why not make out a good, healthy bill of fare that would eliminate Christianity from the blood and bloom out into agnostic daisies, lilies and daffa-downdillies of thought? If the alembic theory is correct, this would be the best method of getting rid of Christianity. But the Colonel's strong points are eloquence and inconsistency. Why appeal to the head of an alembic, when you can get the best results by regulating the hopper? Now, Colonel, give us another taste of your philosophy.

Ingersoll.— In the phenomena of mind, we find the same endless chain of efficient causes. The same mechanical necessity. Every thought must have had an efficient cause. Every motive, every desire, every fear, hope and dream *must have been necessarily produced*. The facts and forces governing thought are as absolute as those governing the motions of the planets. A poem is produced by the forces of nature and is as necessarily and naturally produced as mountains and sea. Every mental operation is the necessary result of certain facts and conditions. ("The Gods," page 55.)

Lambert.— I made this long quotation to enable the reader to see clearly what is your idea of free thought. How can a man holding such a doctrine call himself a freethinker or talk of liberty? Hereafter when you speak of free thought and liberty, your hearers will understand that you speak in a Pickwickian sense, or that you do not mean what you say. Having thus made free thought an impossibility, you have the brass to complain that Christianity "has not been the advocate of free thought!" Persecution is one of your unvarying refrains. Now I ask, with what consistency you complain of persecutions, since, according to your doctrine, the persecutors were as much victims of this unavoidable law as were the victims who died at their hands? What protest can you consistently make against the Inquisition, the thumb screws, the racks and iron boots which you so graphically and minutely describe, since all these are the unavoidable results of a law over which man has no control. Is it not time that you had a sympathetic word for the poor persecutors, those unfortunate victims of your law? Why confine your sympathies to only one class of the victims of Fate? Is it not time that you repudiate your doctrine or stop talking about persecutions? I agree with you that there is no such thing as free thought, but not for the reason given by you.

Ingersoll.— It (Christianity) certainly has not been the advocate of free thought, and what is free thought, and what is freedom worth if the mind be enslaved?

Lambert.— Christianity does not advocate free thought for the reason that there is no such thing in existence. The term is a misnomer, though it is the "harp of a thousand strings" to the bummers of philosophy and gong-men of science. To such gentry the high-sounding phrase, "free-thawet," is irresistible, though the tyro in psychology knows that it is absurd. As the hierophant of agnoticism, you should use your influence to have the word removed from the agnostic vocabulary. The psychologist knows that the intellect, or think machine, is not free; that it is chained to the data given it; that it must *necessarily*, if it act at all, draw conclusions from the data as they are, or as it believes them to be. It may have an incorrect apprehension of the data, and then its conclusions will not accord with the facts, but they will and must accord with the intellect's apprehension of the facts — if the intellect be normal. It cannot say that a part is greater than the whole. If A equals B, and B equals C, it is not free in drawing the conclusion, for it must say that C equals A. If all men are mortal, and John is a man, it must say: John is mortal. The conclusion here is *necessary*, not voluntary. The intellect's inability to say otherwise is precisely that which constitutes its value as an authority in the search after truth. The value, then, of the intellect consists in its *utter lack of freedom*. If the intellect could at will draw a false conclusion, is it not evident that it would lose its rational nature? The highest value of the intellect is found in its irredeemable slavery to data. Now, thought is an act of the intellect, and as the intellect is not free its act or thought is not free, for the act of an agent that acts from necessity is not a free act. Therefore thought is not free, and there is no such thing as free thought or freethinker. What you wanted to say was: Christianity has not been the advocate of liberty or freedom, and then I would have promptly contradicted you.

But if the intellect is not free, what becomes of liberty and human freedom? I answer that it is safe enough. No philosopher, except perhaps some noisy agnostics who destroy liberty, ever dreamed of making the intellect the seat or source of liberty. Philosophers of all ages, Christian and pagan, who admit the existence of liberty, unite in lodging it in the WILL. They make liberty consist in the capacity of the soul to *will* or not to *will*, or to will the contrary, just as it *wills*. Political liberty is the right of every one to follow the bent of his will as long as it does not infringe on the rights of others. Your theory of fate destroys all liberty when it destroys its seat and source, free will. Christianity teaches the freedom of the will; your philosophy denies it. Which is the advocate of liberty?

Ingersoll.— Millions have been sacrificed for exercising their freedom as against the Church.

Lambert.— Here again you forget your own doctrines. How could these millions exercise their freedom as against the Church or anything else if, as you have told us, every motive, every desire, every fear and hope must have been *necessarily* produced, and that all man's thoughts and acts are the result of mechanical necessity?

Ingersoll.— Can we prove that the Church established "human brotherhood" by banishing the Jews from Spain? by driving out the Moors? by the Inquisition? by butchering the Covenanters in Scotland? etc.

Lambert.—No, that is not the way the Christian would prove it. He would prove it by quoting the doctrines of Christ as inculcated by the Church and by historical facts, and not by the fictions you have given above. The Jews and Moors were foreigners and invaders in Spain, as the forces of Maximillian were in Mexico. The Mexicans drove the latter out and executed the Austrian Pretender. We think they did right, and if the Jews and Moors were objectionable to the Spanish people, we see no reason why they should not expel them. The doctrine of Christianity does not imply that we should turn imbeciles and permit a foreign enemy to overrun our country. In any case it was an affair of the Spanish nation and not of Christianity. I notice that when Christians do anything of which you disapprove you attribute it to Christianity, and when Christianity does something you must approve you invariably attribute it to individuals who did it in spite of Christianity. You are sworn to convict Christianity in any case. It is a sad thing when a man permits one idea to take possession of his mind and grow and swell till it drives out all other ideas, or crowds and pushes them out of their normal relations. Such a one is said to have a fixed idea, or to be a man of one idea. You seem to suffer from a chronic nightmare and call it Christianity. Lawrence Sterne, in his "Tristram Shandy," describes this one-idea man under the name "hypothesis." "It is" says he, "the nature of an hypothesis, when once a man has conceived it, that it assimilates everything to itself as proper nourishment, and from the first moment of his begetting it, it generally grows the stronger by everything he sees, hears, reads, or understands." Here Sterne takes you off with the faithfulness of a kodak. I have already spoken of the Inquisition in our last conversation. As to the butchering of the Covenanters, English history tells us that the Scotch people cut each other's throats to a considerable extent and that Oliver Cromwell assisted them with his ability and experience; but how you can charge it to Christianity is what I cannot understand, unless on Sterne's "hypothesis" theory. True, they warred about Christian doctrine, as people war about almost anything.

Ingersoll.— Neither do I believe it true that "we are indebted to Christianity for the advancement of science, art, philosophy, letters and learning."

Lambert.— The fact itself is of more importance than your belief concerning it. Christianity, it is true, did not create science or philosophy, as it did not create the human mind, but it gave the human mind the environments and conditions and supplied it with those principles which made progress in science, philosophy and art possible. Agnostics try to show that Christianity is antagonistic and detrimental to science, art, etc., but in doing so they simply destroy the bridge over which they have passed the stream, or the ladder by which men reached the present elevation on which they stand. Science, in the present sense of the term, never was, and is not now, known in any country outside Christian influence. Christianity did not propose to itself the solution or even the statement of scientific problems, but its doctrines of God's creation, the unity and uniformity of the universe, supply the foundation of all the arts. "In this way," says Professor Lindsay, who suggests this line of thought, "the thought of God, as the Creator and preserver of all things, gives a complete unity to the universe, which pagan thought never reached, and gave the basis for the uniformity of nature which science demands. It was long ere Christianity could force this thought (of unity and uniformity of nature) on the human intelligence, but until it had permeated the whole round of man's intellectual work, it was vain to look for advances in science. It was the task of scholastic theology and philosophy to knead into human thought Christian ideas, and among the rest this idea of the unity and uniformity of nature. When scholasticism had accomplished this task, modern science sprang into being, dependent for its very foundation on that Christianity to which it is supposed to be so bitterly hostile."

It is in this way that science, art, philosophy, letters and learning are indebted to Christianity, plus the encouragement which Christianity has always given.

Ingersoll.—I cheerfully admit that we are indebted to Christianity for some learning.

Lambert.—There is a suspicious cheerfulness about this admission that warns us to keep what the quaint Artemus Ward called a "peeled optic" on what is to follow.

Ingersoll.—And that the human mind has been developed by the discussion of the absurdities and superstitions.

Lambert.—Christianity must decline to accept this crumb of praise, inasmuch as it does not deserve it, not having discussed the subjects you speak of. It left that to scientists, philosophers and theologians, and if there is any credit due at all it is due to them. You are as indiscriminate in your praise as in your blame.

Ingersoll.—Certainly millions and millions—

Lambert.— I have been told you are a very liberal man.

Ingersoll.— Millions and millions have had what might be called mental exercise —

Lambert.— But was it mental exercise? If so, why haggle; if not, why admit?

Ingersoll.— And their minds may have been somewhat broadened by the examination.

Lambert.— But were they broadened? If so, why make the concession limp so? One would imagine you were extracting one of your eye-teeth.

Ingersoll.— By the examination even of these absurdities, contradictions and impossibilities —

Lambert.— What absurdities, contradictions and impossibilities! It is evident you never studied scholastic philosophy, but have found these catch-words in some shallow hand-book of modern philosophy. They smell of index learning. The great French historian, M. Guizot, does not make concessions so gingerly as you do. He says: " Had not the Christian Church existed, the whole world would have been swayed by physical force. She alone exercised moral power. It was the Church which powerfully assisted in forming the character and furthering the development of modern civilization," whose monasteries were, even in the most gloomy period, the schools of Christian philosophy, whose clergy "were active and potent at once in the domain of intellect and in that of reality," and that "the human mind, beaten down by storm, took refuge in the asylum of churches and monasteries." Maitland, speaking of these Christian institutions of learning, says they were "the repositories of learning which then was, and the well springs of the learning which was to be, as nurseries of art and science, giving the stimulus, the means and the reward to invention, and aggregating around them every head that could devise and every hand that could execute."

CHAPTER III.

Ingersoll.— That we are indebted to Christianity for the advance of science seems absurd. What science?

Lambert.— And yet it is a fact. Christianity supplied the foundation of all true science, art and philosophy when it taught man the existence of a Supreme Being, the origin of thought and of things; that this Being designed the universe and willed it to be, and to continue in its acts to conform to that will of His which we call the natural law and Divine Providence. This doctrine of Christianity supplies the human mind with the idea of *design*, with the fact of the *unity* and *uniformity* of the universe, and with the idea of law and order as distinguished from fate and caprice. Now, these ideas of design, unity, uniformity, law and order are at the bottom of all the sciences, arts and philosophies, and no science, art or true philosophy can be constructed or worked out without them as a starting-point. I do not say that Christianity originated these ideas, for they exist in a manner more or less obscure in the minds of all men; but it sanctioned with divine authority, illuminated, illustrated and inculcated them until the intellectual activity of the Christian world grew accustomed to them as the data of reasoning, whether in the physical, moral, ethical or intellectual world. I call your attention to the fact that, for a thousand years, no progress has been made on the face of the earth in science, art, or philosophy, except where Christian thought prevails.

Reflect on this fact and see if you can discover any cause for it other than the inspirations of Christianity, which has spurred the human mind to an activity in all directions unknown to the world outside the circle of its influence.

The Christian Church did not confine herself to this. When she rose to influence in the Roman

Empire, she began to send out missionaries to all the peoples to what is now known as Europe, to the northern barbaric pagan tribes, to Spain, France, Germany, England and Ireland, and wherever they went cathedrals, schools and religious houses arose and communities formed about them. These became the centres of peaceful employment, education and civilization. They were the asylums of learning at times when all Europe was a battlefield, when, owing to the dissolution of the Roman Empire, nation contended with nation, and the Northern invaders swarmed down over Central and Southern Europe at different times under Alaric, Genseric, and Attila, and threatened to sweep away what then existed of civilization. It is to these times that M. Guizot alluded when he wrote: "Had not the Christian Church existed, the whole world would have been swayed by physical force." The Church converted and civilized those barbaric conquerors. In these schools, established all over Europe by the missionaries, was preserved the literature of the past. The members of the religious orders spent their lives in translating into the newly forming languages the Scriptures, the classics, the histories and scientific works of Greece and Rome. Were it not for their labors, all these would be as unknown to us as the literature of the Pelasgic

Greeks and of Egypt prior to the Shepherd Kings.

To these Christian teachers we owe the works of Homer, Aristotle, Ptolemy, Euclid, in fact all the Greek and Latin authors extant, for had they not devoted their lives to the preservation of them, the revolutions and invasions that swept, wave after wave, over Europe would have left no vestige of them. In this great work these men were inspired by the genius of Christianity. The unbiased historian of learning and civilization in Europe will recognize what learning in all its branches owes to Christianity. In these cathedrals and monastic schools were collected and preserved all the great libraries which had been copied and recopied by tireless pens — for the art of printing and multiplying books had not yet been discovered. From these schools sprang the great universities.

The genius of Christianity encourages labor in all the sciences.

Ingersoll.— What sciences? Christianity was certainly the enemy of astronomy.

Lambert.— All of them. But as you mention astronomy, let us take that science as an illustration and sketch its steps from the Middle Ages up to the present. In the fifth century the Ptolemaic system of astronomy had taken possession of the European mind. All reasoning on the subject was based on that system. And, strange to say, it explained all the phenomena observed up to the time of Nicolaus Copernicus.

Running our finger down the almanac of time, we strike a name in the *seventh* century — the venerable Bede, the father of English history, a monk and a saint. A man whom the great English statesman, Edmund Burke, from the loftiness of his genius, styled "The father of English literature," and of whom Mr. Turner observes: "He collected and taught more natural truths than any Roman writer had yet accomplished, and his works display an advance, not a retrogression, in science." This man taught that the true shape of the earth was globular, and attributed to this fact the irregularity of our days and nights. He explained the ebb and flow of the tides by the attractive power of the moon, and pointed out the error of supposing that all the waters of the ocean rise at the same moment. He showed that the sun is eclipsed by the intervention of the moon, and the moon by that of the earth. He condemned judicial astrology as false and pernicious.

It seems to me, Colonel, that this old monk's head was somewhat level. Is it not strange that he was not drawn and quartered, or that Christianity did not pour hot lead into his ears, or cut off his eyelids, or fit him with a neat pair of iron boots. He died a beautiful death, which I will speak of, if you remind me, when we come to talk of Voltaire's death, about which you have made some agnostic blunders. Cuthbert, one of Bede's disciples, says of him : "I can declare with truth, that never saw I with my eyes, or heard I with my ears, of any man so indefatigable in giving thanks to God. After study he always applied himself to prayer." I am somewhat puzzled here to tell whether his case was one of science plus holiness or holiness plus science. As you are strong in minus and plus precision, you might help me out.

Run your finger a little further down the line of time and we hit on another monk, an Irishman by the name of Feargil, or O'Farrell, which in Latin, you know, is Virgilius, and in English, Virgil. Wonder if the Mantuan bard had not a drop of Milesian blood in him? But that, by the way. This Irish monk taught the existence of the antipodes. He got into trouble about it, of course. The Church hauled him up, as usual, and made an example of him, it, not having hot lead or iron boots handy, made him Bishop of Salzburg.

A little further down the line we come across Alcuin, another churchman. He taught in Paris in the latter half of the *eighth* century in the time of

Charlemagne, who used to consult him on astronomical questions. In the year 798 the king and his academicians felt great anxiety in consequence of the erratic movements of the planet Mars, whose disappearance for a whole year puzzled them very much. They asked an explanation of Alcuin. In his reply he said: "What has now happened to Mars is frequently observed of all the other planets, viz., that they remain longer under the horizon than is stated in the books of the ancients. The rising and the setting of the stars vary from the observations of those who live in the southern and eastern parts of the world, where the masters chiefly flourished who have set forth the laws of the universe." It is evident from these words that Alcuin was acquainted with the globular form of the earth and the phenomena depending upon it. He was a scientist in all its branches, a man of rare genius and great piety. Was not that strange?

This man whose eagle eye could take in the universe did not lose his head in the physical sciences or in the classic literature of Rome and Greece, of which he was a master. Nor was he puffed up with pride like a frog with chronic dyspepsia — as are so many of our modern scientists and their agnostic gong-men. He could give good advice. He once wrote to a young nobleman in this style: "Seek to adorn your noble rank with noble deeds. *Let humanity be in your heart, and truth on your lips*, and let your life be a pattern of integrity, so that God may be pleased to prosper your days." There is more wisdom in these few lines, Colonel, than in all the philosophy, so called, that you ever uttered. It would improve you and your flatulent followers greatly if you followed his advice. I cannot resist the temptation to quote some more from this man's writings. There is a healthy, vigorous atmosphere about them that one needs after rising from a perusal of your wisdom. Of course, being a man of genius and a scientist, Alcuin could not escape scot free the persecutions of the Christian Church. But it being a day off at the Inquisition, and lead and iron boots being costly,— owing, perhaps, to a high protective McKinley tariff,— the Church could not take full revenge on him, so they only made him an Abbot — Abbot of St. Martin's in France. From this gloomy prison or penitentiary, or what you may call it, he wrote a letter to Charlemagne, in which he tells how he passed the tedious hours of his imprisonment. "I spend my time in the halls of St. Martin, teaching the noble youths under my care. To some I serve out the honey of Holy Scriptures. Others I essay to intoxicate with the wine of ancient literature. One class I nourish with the apples of grammatical studies, and to the eyes of others I display the order of the shining orbs that adorn the azure heavens." To some students who asked him the end of philosophy and how to attain it, he replied: "It will be easy to show you the way to wisdom, provided you seek it purely for God's sake, to preserve the purity of your own soul, and for the love of virtue." "Master," continued they, "raise us up from the earth where our ignorance now detains us, and lead us to those heights of science where you passed your own early years. The poets would seem to tell us that the sciences are the true banquets of the gods." To which he answered: "We read of Wisdom which is spoken of by the mouth of Solomon, that she built herself a house and hewed out seven pillars. Now, although these pillars represent the seven gifts of the Holy Ghost and the seven Sacraments of the Church, we may also discern in them the *seven liberal arts*, grammar, rhetoric, dialectics, arithmetic, geometry, music and astronomy, which are like so many steps on which philosophers expend their labors, and have obtained the honors of eternal renown." And this in the eighth century, mind you! In the mind of this great man there does not appear any antagonism between religion and science. His thoughts are as refreshing as the country air laden with the sweet odors of the grass and the trees after a gentle shower.

Ingersoll.—Christianity was certainly an enemy of astronomy, and I believe that it was Dr. Draper who said that astronomy took her revenge, so that not a star that glitters in all the heavens bears a Christian name.

Lambert.—The remark is a very silly one, whoever made it. The Romans, and through them the peoples of Europe, received their astronomical knowledge, limited as it was, from the Greeks, Pythagoras, Hipparchus and Ptolemy, and with it the Greek nomenclature. The Almagest of Ptolemy was the text-book for centuries in Christian Europe. Christian scholars knew the confusion that is caused by changing the terminology of a science, and therefore retained the Greek terms. Had they discarded them, you would have complained. They retained them, and you sneer that astronomy took her revenge! You are like the Frenchman who was to be hanged, neither a long nor a short rope would suit him. But let us go back to our illustration. We stopped at Alcuin. In 314 we find Musva, a Christian physician, teaching astronomy to Al-Mamun, the son of Harun-al-Raschid, King of Babylon.

We now come to Gerbert, in the *tenth* century, that mediæval time when darkness was at its highest concentration. The diversified character of his acquirements made this man of genius the wonder of the world in the eyes of his contemporaries, and the natural sciences were his special attraction. He wrote several treaties on astronomy, mathematics, geometry, the formation of the astrolabe, the quadrant and the sphere. He made a clock for Otho III. which he regulated by the polar star, which he observed *through a kind of tube* — evidently a primitive telescope. In teaching astronomy he used various instruments, among them a *globe with its poles oblique to the horizon.* He introduced the system of decimal notation, the miscalled Arabic numerals, to Christian Europe. But of that further on. A man of such prodigious activity of mind would, as you may naturally suppose, attract the cold, octopus eye of Christianity. He did. He was brought to Rome. He was helpless and entirely in their power and they — cut his tongue out, poured hot lead into his ears, stretched him on a rack and applied the iron boot? — Oh, no, they made him Pope and called him Sylvester the Second.

We come now to Albertus Magnus, who, says Humboldt in his "Cosmos," "was equally active and influential in promoting the study of natural science and of the Aristotelian philosophy." He decided that the Milky Way was a vast assemblage of stars,— this before the invention of the telescope,— and that the figures on the moon, before his time supposed to be reflections of the seas and mountains of the earth, were the configurations of the moon's own surface. He describes the antipodes and the countries they comprise, and explains why they do not fall off, saying, "when we speak of the *lower* hemispheres this must be understood merely as relatively to ourselves." M. Meyer, speaking of Albertus, says: "All honor to the man who made such astonishing progress in the science of nature as to find no one, I will not say to surpass but even to equal him for the space of three centuries." As usual, you may be sure, the Church got hold of him. He was taken to Rome and made the Pope's consulting theologian.

Roger Bacon, a monk, was another scientist of the Middle Ages. Of him the astronomer Bouvier says: "One of the most extraordinary minds of that or any age, made some valuable suggestions on the construction of astronomical instruments. He also proposed a reformation of the calendar three hundred years before any corrections were made in it."

In the early part of the fifteenth century we come across the name of Nicholas de Cusa. In his work entitled "De Docta Ignorantia," we find the following: "It is manifest to us that the earth *is truly in motion*, although it does not appear to us, since we do not apprehend motion except by something fixed. For if anyone were in a boat, in the middle of the river, ignorant that the water was flowing, and not seeing the banks, how could he apprehend that the boat was moving? And thus since every one, whether he be in the earth, or in the sun, or in any other star, thinks that he is in an immovable centre, and that everything else is moving, he would assign different poles for himself, others as being in the sun, and others in the moon, and so on for the rest. Whence the machine of the world is as if it had its centre everywhere and its circumference nowhere." Here we have the origin of the phrase "*E pur si muove,*" "*and yet it moves,*" attributed to Galileo. The infatuation that makes the shallow gong-men of science attribute to Galileo the origin of the doctrine of the earth's movement is unaccountable. You will naturally be interested in the fate of poor de Cusa. He was lured to Rome and made a Cardinal.

Then comes Copernicus, who revolutionized astronomy in 1543, by his celebrated work, "De Revolutionibus Orbium Cœlestium," which, strange to say, he dedicated to Pope Paul III. He put his work under the protection of the Pope that his august character and patronage might shield him from the ridicule of contemporary *scientists*, who, he feared, would consider him a crank. In the dedication he said: "I must be allowed to believe that as soon as what I have written about the motion of the earth will be known, cries of indignation will be uttered against me. Besides, I am not so much in love with my own ideas as not to take into account what others will think of them;" then, though the thoughts of a philosopher follow a different direction from those of the generality of men, because he proposes to himself to search after truth, as far as God has allowed it to human reason: "I do not think, however, that I ought to regret opinions which seem to differ from mine. . . . All these motives, as the fear of becoming an object of laughter on account of the novelty and the (apparent) absurdity of my view, had almost made me give up my undertaking. But friends, among whom are the Cardinal Schomberg and Tiedman Giese, Bishop of Kulm, succeeded in conquering my repugnance. The latter particularly *insisted most earnestly* that I should publish this book which I had kept by on the stocks, not nine, but nearly thirty-six years."

There are three important points to be noticed in this letter of Copernicus: —

1st.— That it was the *scientists* of his time he feared, and not the Church. The scientists would be indignant and laugh at him.

2nd.— His repugnance to publish his great work, that was to revolutionize astronomy, was overcome by two churchmen — Cardinal Schomberg and the Bishop of Kulm — the latter of whom *insisted earnestly* that it should be published. So both the discovery and the promulgation of the modern system of astronomy were due to these Christian clergymen. There was no agnosticism or infidelity about it.

3rd.— The tone of the whole letter shows the true Christian humility of a great scientific genius. How different from the loquacious egotism of some modern scientific smatterers who, when they think they have discovered some new theory, go about cutting pigeon wings and cackling like a hen that has laid an egg. This sets the chanticleers and street-corner-quack-medicine-venders of science agoing, and the clatter is kept up, till the theory explodes on their hands, before they have had time to get at Moses about it. Their measure of the value of a discovery is how hard they think it will hit Moses and revelation.

Following Copernicus comes such Christian names as Tycho Brahe, Galileo, Euler, Kepler, Descartes, Huygens, Newton, Leibnitz. All these were masters and there is not an agnostic among them. Is not that strange?

Now we can, if you wish, take any of the other sciences, and we can point out great men in the Christian past who worked zealously in the cause of science, and talked much less than the average agnostic. You will say that their labors and discoveries were in spite of Christianity, and I will say that you had better go over to the Brooklyn Navy Yard and tell the marines about it.

Ingersoll.— Can it be said that the Church has been the friend of geology, or of any true philosophy? Let me show how this is impossible.

Lambert. — That will be interesting. By all means proceed.

Ingersoll.— The Church accepts the Bible as an inspired book.

Lambert.— That is correct. Now, then.

Ingersoll.— Then the only object is to find its meaning.

Lambert.— That is certainly the first object, but it does not follow that it is the *only* one. But let that pass; go on.

Ingersoll.—And if that meaning is opposed to any result that the human mind may have reached, the meaning stands and the result reached by the mind must be abandoned.

Lambert.—The Christian believes that the Supreme Being who inspired the Bible is the same God who created nature, life and intelligence, and that this *Primum Philosophicum* and Source of existences as well as revelation cannot contradict Himself and say one thing in revelation and the contrary in nature. This is the basis on which the Christian begins his reasoning, and from this he concludes that the true meaning of the Bible and the true results of science cannot contradict each other. To the Christian, then, your hypothesis bears on its very face an absurdity. This he sees directly by his Christian instinct. Hence, when in scientific investigations he comes across results or supposed results which are in contradiction to what he thinks to be the meaning of the Bible, he pauses and reflects, and instead of saying "the Bible contradicts science," he says, "either I have not understood the Bible rightly or I have not understood science correctly; and before I can affirm a contradiction I must readjust and reconsider my data. What I have taken to be the meaning of the Bible may not be its meaning, and what I have taken as a result of science may be only the result of a miscalculation somewhere; and before I can assert a contradiction between them I must *know* the meaning of the Bible and have the *last word* of science on the subject. I know that this universe is but the thought of God projected into existence by His creative act, and that His word does not contradict His world."

This is the way in which a philosophic Christian mind would proceed, and not agnostic-wise draw the sword of Falstaff on men in buckram and kendal green. I have said the Christian will see the absurdity of your hypothesis at a glance, but a careful analysis of it will make this all the more clear. The sophistry of your argument lurks in the indefinite phrases, "Any result that the human mind may have reached" and "the result reached by human mind." Now, what do you mean by "results reached by the human mind?" Do you mean results reached a thousand years ago? or those up to the present moment? or those to be reached one hundred or five hundred years hence? The history of the race is a history of changes in what you call "results reached by the mind," reached only to be changed on more and broader data. The history of science is the history of corrections and changes of results reached by the human mind. These results, then, to be of value in a comparison, must be *ultimate* results, and be *known* to be such, otherwise we cannot know but future experience may afford data which will make it necessary for the human mind to throw aside present results and adopt new ones.

I speak, of course, of the physical sciences. If you say you take present results for a comparison with the Bible I will object until you prove that the present results are ultimate; that no possible future discoveries can change them; that they are complete and fixed forever and nothing more can ever be known — in a word, that science has uttered its last word on that subject. Of course, you know that this proof is impossible, and yet my objection is legitimate and logical. Until you demonstrate that present results are ultimate and forever fixed, your making them the test of the truth of the Bible is absurd.

To impress on you the importance of that last word or scientific ultimate, I will give an illustration. Suppose yourself to be retrojected to the days of Ptolemy. Your mind would be as full of the Ptolemaic system of astronomy as it is now of that of Copernicus. You meet a Christian from Thebes, say, and you would reason with him thus: Your Bible is wrong. Why, sir? Because it is in contradiction with the results reached by the human mind. The Christian asks: "Are the results the last on the subject?" You would say, of course, "They are," just as you say it now.

Now let us suppose that Christian to be brought down to our time. He hears you talk learnedly, as it were, on astronomy. "Hello, my astronomical friend, are you not the scientist I met on the banks of the Nile one thousand eight hundred years ago? What are the latest results reached by the human mind? Here is my Bible — I did not change it to suit your 'results reached by the human mind,' and I am glad I did not, for now I would have to change it again to suit the new set of 'results reached by the human mind.' Now, my ancient friend, tell me, if I change my Bible to suit the new 'results,' will you promise I will not have to change it again the next time we meet five hundred years hence?" What would you say?

When you can assure the Christian that your "results reached by the human mind" are fixed, finished, complete and unalterable, you will be ready to use them as a test of the meaning of the Bible. But as you cannot give any such assurance, you cannot get at his Bible. The obstacle in your way is insurmountable, for you must admit that science is progressive, and the "results reached by the human mind " must go on a sort of sliding scale to keep up with the progress, and this progress will continue until the Angel of Eternity calls the muster roll of time. Therefore, at no given time can you say that any given result is the last word of science on the subject.

But you will ask: Is not the Copernican system sufficiently established to test the truth of the Scriptures by it? I answer no, and for the following reasons: Science has not yet passed an ultimate judgment on it! It is true that the system accounts for all the astronomical phenomena observed up to the present time. But this fact does not demonstrate its truth, for the Ptolemaic system accounted for all the phenomena to the satisfaction of scientists up to the time of Copernicus, who excogitated what we believe to be a more perfect system, and rendered incalculable service to science by enabling it to account for all the phenomena observed in the new fields opened up by the telescope and other more perfect instruments used in astronomy.

Now as the Ptolemaic scientist would have erred in saying that science had said its last word in formulating that ancient system, so the scientist of to-day risks falling into the same error when he asserts that the astronomical science has given its ultimate judgment in the Copernican formula. All he is justified in saying is that this formula is the *latest*, but not the last word science may have to say.

But has it not been demonstrated? No, it has not! To demonstrate the truth of the Copernican system three things are necessary: First, that it account for all phenomena observed up to the present. Second, that it can account for all possible phenomena that greater experience, wider observation and more perfect instruments may open up to human knowledge. No scientist of to-day can say that it can do this, for proof of this is, in the nature of things, impossible, as a moment's reflection will make evident. And, third, that no other possible system can account for the phenomena of the science, past, present and future. This requirement is equally unprovable. Therefore the truth of the Copernican system has not been demonstrated.

But is it not true? Here I will for just once play the agnostic and say I don't know. This is the only world I was ever in and I am somewhat provincial, at least I think I am, but I also think I don't know for certain; that is to say, I think that I think that I think that I t-h-i-n-k — Ah, Colonel, quick, your smelling salts — ah — I'm better now — but I'll not try to ride an agnostic hobby again, it jolts worse than a wild mustang.

Of what value, then, is the system? Will you reject it in the face of the science and learning of the day? No, I look on the system as a miracle of human genius, as of immense value to mankind, and that the probability of its truth is as a million to one, but as long as that *one* remains the truth of the system is not demonstrated. This *one* possibility against it must be eliminated before the system is demonstrated. The presence of this one possibility against the million probabilities, however, does not prevent the system from being useful for all the affairs of life in this world. Why then may we not compare its results with the Scripture? I will tell you. The uttered word of the Supreme Being, the Absolute Truth, must be *necessarily* true, for it is a contradiction in terms to say or think that the Perfect Being could utter an untruth. Here, then, we have a *necessary* truth, a truth that *cannot not-be*. In the Copernican system we have a *most probable* truth, a million or ten million to one — that fatal one which makes the Copernican probable truth one that *can not-be*.

This astronomic probable truth is empirical, experimental, as all the results or conclusions of the physical sciences, from their very nature, must be. The difference, then, between these two truths is this. The former is a truth that cannot not-be, necessary truth. The latter is a truth that can not-be, a contingent truth. It is evident that the former is of a higher order than the latter.

Now, with this explanation we can see how absurd it is to make a truth of a lower order the measure of a truth of a higher order, or to make a probable result of science the measure and touchstone of the veracity of the Supreme Being, if these two kinds of truth should appear to come in collision. I say, should *appear* to come in collision, for a real collision between the true results of science and the uttered word of God is impossible, since the Supreme Being is the origin and source of both kinds of truth — the revealed and natural — both kinds of existences, intelligences and matter, and He, the Absolute Truth, cannot contradict Himself.

The conclusion from all this is that when there appears to be contradictions between the inspired word of God and the true results of science, we must conclude they are only apparent, not real. And when a real contradiction exists, science must readjust its data. To illustrate this let us suppose that the Scripture in so many words clearly and explicitly condemned the Copernican system as erroneous. What then? Why I would immediately conclude that in the probabilities of ten million to one, the one had won, and that science should direct its energy to working out the true system that would account for all phenomena past, present and to come. But, as a matter of fact, the so-called contradictions harped on by the agnostics are only men in buckram and kendal green.

Now after this long, but necessary digression, let us go back to Mr. Ingersoll's argument, which is that it is impossible that the Church has been the friend of science.

Ingersoll.—Let me show you how this is impossible. The Church accepts the Bible as inspired.

Lambert.—Yes, I admit all that and that if the true meaning of the Bible contradicts a "result reached by the human mind," that result must be abandoned and the human mind must try again, for it knows it makes a great many blunders.

Just here it strikes me that in the long explanation above I left out one possible meaning which you may have attached to the phrase, "results reached by the human mind." You may have meant what Christian philosophers call the *sensus communus*, or common consent of mankind. If you meant this, it is equally useless to you, for the common consent of mankind does not affirm the Copernican system. On the contrary, the great majority of mankind in the past as in the present knew nothing whatever about it; "the results reached by the human mind" tells them nothing about it. It is only within the pale and influence of Christian civilization that the Copernican system is known and taught. This fact probably never occurred to you. But let us return to the point from which we have wandered — by the way, what a vagrant spirit takes possession of one when meditating on agnostic philosophy! Your point was to prove that the Church plus Bible was an enemy of the sciences. But as we have been rambling somewhat, suppose you state it again that we may have another look at it.

CHAPTER IV.

Ingersoll.— Can it be said that the Church is the friend of geology or of any true philosophy? Let me show you how this is impossible. The Church accepts the Bible as an inspired book. Then the only object is to find its meaning; and, if that meaning is opposed to any result that the human mind may have reached, the meaning stands and the result reached by the mind must be abandoned.

Lambert.— The full force of the argument will be better seen if we throw the reasoning into the form of a syllogism; it would then stand thus: —

Whatever causes the "results reached by the

human mind" to be abandoned, is not a friend of true philosophy. But the Church plus the Bible causes the " results reached by the human mind" to be abandoned; therefore the Church plus the Bible is not a friend of true philosophy. This draws out the full force of the argument and presents it in logical form. It must be admitted that thus presented it looks somewhat formidable. It is an agnostic battery loaded to the muzzle. There is no way to get around it, so we must attack it in front and take it by storm, for taken it must be, or we must retire beyond its reach; in a word, we must retreat, but as that cannot be thought of for a moment, we must rig up some sort of a syllogistic Krupp gun that will blow it into pieces. This gun will be in the shape of another syllogism, and stands thus: —

Whatever causes the " results reached by the human mind" to be abandoned, is no friend of true philosophy.

But Copernicus caused the " results reached by the human mind" in astronomy to be abandoned. Therefore Copernicus was no friend of astronomy.

Now, Colonel, are you prepared to accept this logical result of your line of argument and lower the flag on your battery? No! Very well, I'll give you another shot.

Ampère caused the "results reached by the human mind" on electricity to be abandoned. Therefore Ampère was not a friend of science.

Do you surrender yet? Not yet? Well, here goes again.

Lavoisier, by exploding the Phlogiston theory of chemistry, caused the "results reached by the human mind" to be abandoned. Therefore Lavoisier was not a friend of science.

You don't lower your flag yet? Well, here goes again.

Champollion caused the "results reached by the human mind" on Egyptology to be abandoned. Therefore he was not a friend of science.

Dr. Young caused the "results reached by the human mind" on the theory of light to be abandoned. Therefore he was not a friend of science.

Newton, Franklin, Edison caused the results of the hu — Ah, that is right, but you should have come down sooner. In fact the great scientists are great precisely because they caused the scientific results of the human mind to be abandoned and new results to be accepted. Now, Colonel, this skirmish makes it clear as "a result of the human mind" that even if I were to admit that the Church plus the Bible caused "the results reached by the human mind" to be abandoned, it would not follow that the Church plus the Bible was not a friend of science and true philosophy. That is the way your fine-spun sophisms go off in vapor under analysis. Yet, strange as it may seem, there are some people who think, in the simplicity of their hearts, that you are a logician.

Ingersoll.— For hundreds of years the Bible was the standard, and whenever anything was asserted in any science contrary to the Bible, the Church immediately denounced the scientist.

Lambert.— It is strange how far a mind, once thrown from its equilibrium by blind unreasoning prejudice can go. There is a likeness between love and hatred in this, that when a man permits either passion to take full control of him he flings calm reason to the winds, gives the rein and bends all his energies to the spur, and like one in a mad delirium dashes onward, he knows not and cares not whither — only that it is onward. Shakespeare with his master hand describes this state of mind in the words of baffled Florizel in "Winter's Tale:"—

Florizel: I
Am heir to my affection.
    Camillo: Be advis'd.
    Florizel: I am; and by my fancy: if my reason
Will thereto be obedient, I have reason;
If not, my senses, better pleas'd with madness,
Do bid it welcome.

Camillo: This is desperate, sir.
Florizel: So call it; but it does fulfill my vow:
I needs must think it honesty.

For hundreds of years the Bible was the standard.

No sane man need be told that the Bible was never the standard of the physical sciences. It is a book that deals with man's spiritual and moral nature. It makes no claim to be a treatise on science, nor was any such claim ever made for it by Jew or Christian. In the first part it treats of the origin of things — a field into which the physical sciences cannot enter, for these treat of things as they find them in existence. Part of it relates to Jewish political, civil and domestic life and history; another part treats of the moral law, and still another of prophecy, but no part is devoted to the physical sciences. It is the same with the Christian Church. She does not and never did teach the physical sciences, for such is not her mission, though she encouraged in her schools the study of them.

And whenever anything was asserted in any science contrary to the Bible, the Church immediately denounced the scientist.

One who puts himself forward as a teacher and reformer and flaunts his crude notions aggressively and offensively in the face of a patient Christian people should have at least some show of respect for public opinion and historic truth. Did the Church denounce Bede, Alcuin, Gerbert, Albertus Magnus, Celio Calcagnini, De Cusa, Novara, Da Vinci, Torricelli?

The Church was the friend of all the sciences, and of letters and arts as well. I ask, in the words of the Archbishop of Malines: Who founded the universities of Oxford and Cambridge, in England? The Popes. Who founded the universities of Paris, Bologna, Ferrara, Salamanca, Coimbra, Alcala, Heidelberg, Prague, Cologne, Vienna, Louvaine, and Copenhagen? The Popes. Who instituted the professorships of the Greek, Hebrew, Arabic and Chaldaic languages at Paris, Oxford, Bologna and Salamanca? Pope Clement the Fifth. By whom, during two centuries, were sustained, encouraged, recompensed the works of savants which finally lead to the knowledge of the system of the world? The Popes and Cardinals.

When was the system of the earth's movement adopted and first taught? At Rome in 1425 by Nicholas de Cusa, professor in the Roman University, forty-eight years before the birth of Copernicus, and one hundred and thirty-nine years before Galileo was born. De Cusa at that time defended the system of the earth's movement in a work dedicated to Cardinal Julian Cesarini. Pope Nicholas V. raised De Cusa to the Cardinalate. Again it was at Rome, toward the year 1500, that Copernicus explained and defended this system before an audience of two thousand scholars. He was made Canon of Koenigsberg. Celio Calcagnini, who taught the system of De Cusa and Copernicus in Italy about 1518, was appointed apostolic prothonotary by Clement VIII., and confirmed in this position of honor by Paul III. It was to Paul III. that Copernicus dedicated his work "De Revolutionibus Orbium Cœlestium." It was a Pope who used his utmost endeavors to place Kepler in the University of Bologna. The Church never fears the light. She knows and teaches that the light of reason and the light of faith come from the same source; that one of these truths will never contradict the other, and that among the proofs of revelation we must not forget its harmony with the sciences. From Clement of Alexandria and Origen to Descartes, Leibnitz, Pascal, Kepler and De Maistre, to say nothing of our contemporaries, science and faith have dwelt together in the greatest minds of Christendom. This list of *historical* facts is enough to overthrow all your glib statements on the subject.

But what about Galileo?

As a doctrine of the movement of the earth was taught before Galileo was born by men who were promoted to high positions in the Church, it is very natural to suppose that if Galileo got into difficulties with the authorities it was not for teaching the heliocentric theory of astronomy, but for *plus something else.*

No modern astronomer with a reputation to lose would now dream of endorsing the arguments of Galileo for the diurnal motion of the earth. And the heliocentric theory was publicly taught by Copernicus and others before he was born. He was, however, a man of genius, and notwithstanding the many squabbles his quick temper and sarcastic tongue and pen got him into, he was pensioned by his friend Pope Urban VIII., and he continued to receive that pension until the day of his death. This naked fact is enough to silence the cry that the Church is the enemy of science. The enemies of Galileo were the *scientists* of his own time, who, like many of their modern brethren, were stiff-necked and wise in their own conceit. He would have saved himself much trouble if he had taken the advice of his friend Monsignor Dini. "Write freely," said that friend, "but keep out of the sacristy." This is equally good advice for the modern scientists, who, not satisfied with their retorts and gases, must needs be theologians, metaphysicians, interpreters of scripture and critics of Moses. No man can know all things.

Ingersoll.— Certainly, Christianity has done nothing for art.

Lambert.— This is one of those loose, sweeping statements which are found scattered with a liberal hand in all your writings. It is not clear what you mean by art. But I will suppose you mean music, painting, sculpture, architecture, and ask you to look over the face of the earth to-day and point out those countries where these arts have been most cultivated since the advent of Christianity. Go from pole to pole or follow the sun's light as it sweeps like a wing of fire around the globe, and when you find where these arts flourish, you will find that you are in Christian lands. Now, as they have died out everywhere else but within the pale of Christianity, we must conclude on general principles that Christianity nourished and encouraged their cultivation and supplied to men of genius higher and nobler ideals than the pagan world knew. This general argument is enough to contradict your statement. But if we were to enter into the history of the progress of these arts, the fallacy of what you say would become still more apparent.

Ingersoll.— The early Christians destroyed all the marbles of Greece and Rome they could lay their violent hands on.

Lambert.— When we consider the many revolutions, social upheavals and invasions from the barbaric North that swept over Southern Europe, we are surprised that there still remain so many magnificent specimens of Greek sculpture. You seem to be ignorant of all these causes of destruction of works of art. You forget to mention the destruction of art by the iconoclastic followers of the Crescent. For you there seems to be but one cause of all evils, Christianity. But if what you say be true, how comes it that there are so many works of Greek art preserved in Christian countries as precious heirlooms to-day. The dying Gladiator of which Byron wrote, the Marble Faun immortalized by Hawthorne, the Laocoon, and a multitude of other works of arts to be found in Rome, Naples and other cities, stand as silent witnesses of the falseness of your assertion. Christians got their hands on all of them and preserved them. Had you seen the art museums of Rome, Naples and other cities in Europe, you would have been less profligate of speech.

Ingersoll.— There have been many artists who were Christians, but they were not artists because they were Christians.

Lambert.— What a profound observation. Their education was Christian. The arts were taught in the Christian schools and universities, where men of genius received their instruction. The masterpieces of Michael Angelo, Raphael, Murillo, Canova and hundreds of others were made at the instance of Church dignitaries, and these masters were ever honored and encouraged by the Church. What would these great men have been if brought up in Turkey under the Mohammedan religion? They had genius, but genius depends for its development on favorable environments, and these the Christian Church surrounded them with, and it is to these, and their genius, that they owe their achievements and their fame. No one but an agnostic mole can read the history of Christian Europe without recognizing that art as known now is the result of Christian influence and encouragement.

Ingersoll.— But there were Christians who were not artists.

Lambert.— Here is another profound observation. It shows you are a deep thinker and a keen observer,

Ingersoll.— It cannot be said that art is born of any creed.

Lambert.— Another ponderous observation. But who ever insinuated that art is born of any creed? Is it not to you an inexplicable fact that art flourishes now only where the Christian creed prevails? Where is art outside of Christendom? Did these questions never suggest themselves to you in your profound meditations?

Ingersoll.— The mode of expression may be determined, and probably is, to a certain degree, by the belief of the artist, but not his artistic perception and feeling.

Lambert.— The Church never claimed to supply men with genius — artistic perception and feeling. But she did supply those whom nature had made artists with noble and sublime ideals and conceptions, which their genius realized to the senses. In other words, Christianity determined the mode of expression; opened new fields to the appreciative eye of the artist, and kindled his ambition to put forth his best efforts.

Ingersoll.— So Galileo did not make his discoveries because he was a Christian, but in spite of it.

Lambert.— By discoveries I suppose you mean his teaching that the earth moves. That was not his discovery, for it was taught over a century before he was born. Do you mean his theory of tides? The astronomer of to-day only smiles with indulgence on that theory as childish. Shakespeare, who made no pretension as a scientist, knew more about the true theory of the tides than Galileo, for in 1611, some time before the latter published his " Dialogues," he made Camillo say:—

> "Swear his thought over
> By each particular star in Heaven, and
> By all their influences, you may as well
> Forbid the sea for to obey the moon,
> As, or by oath, remove or counsel, shake
> The fabric of his folly."

The astronomer now knows that the theory indicated by the Bard of Avon is the true theory, while that of Galileo was erroneous. Then what discoveries did Galileo make that contradicted the Bible or his creed? Was it the invention of the telescope? But he did not invent it. Was it the discovery of the moons of Jupiter? But what is there in the moons of Jupiter contrary to the Bible or to Galileo's creed? What a heap of miserable, ignorant chaff goes under the name of knowledge. As Shakespeare says:

> "I had rather be a tick in a sheep than such a valiant ignorance." (Troilus and Cressida.)

CHAPTER V.

Ingersoll.—Kepler did not discover or announce what are known as the "Three Laws" because he was a Christian, but, as I said about Galileo, in spite of his creed.

Lambert.—What is there in the laws of Mr. Kepler against his creed? Let us see. The first law is that: *The planets revolve about the sun in ellipses, having the sun in one of the foci.* Will you point out wherein the law contradicts the Scriptures? Copernicus, and after him Galileo, believed the planets revolved about the sun in circles, but I find no text of scripture that says they don't revolve in ellipses, and therefore cannot see what it had to do with Kepler's creed. The second law is that: *If a line be drawn from the centre of the sun to any planet, that line, as it is carried forward by the planet, will sweep over equal areas in equal portions of time.* Now, I cannot find anything from Genesis to Revelations speaking of the relation between the movement of radius vector and time. Please point this out in your next lecture. The third law is that: *The squares of the periodic times of the planets are as the cubes of their mean distances from the sun.* I can see nothing in Kepler's Bible or creed that treats of these dynamic laws. There is nothing in either about the cubes or squares or mean distances from the sun. It is a pity there is no one with the genius of Kepler to calculate your mean — very mean — distance from the truth when you discuss Christianity.

Ingersoll.— Every Christian who has really found out and demonstrated and clung to a fact inconsistent with the absolute inspiration of the Scriptures, has done so certainly without the assistance of his creed.

Lambert.— You here, as usual, assume too much. I deny that any Christian or any one else has ever found out and demonstrated a fact inconsistent with the absolute inspiration of the Scriptures. With this denial before you, you must, if you pretend to be a logician, prove your statement. To do this three things are necessary: First, you must prove that the so-called "fact" is a demonstrated fact; and second, you must prove that you have the true meaning, not your interpretation, of the inspired Book; and lastly, that there is a real, not merely an apparent, contradiction. But all these difficulties you skip over with the ease and dexterity of a French dancing master, and assume it all to be done. You are not reasoning, you are only talking.

Ingersoll.— When our ancestors were burning each other to please God —

Lambert.— You should say "under pretense of pleasing God." They followed their ambitions and passions as men have done before and will do on one pretense or another till Gabriel blows his trumpet.

Ingersoll.— When they were ready to destroy a man with sword and flame for teaching the rotundity of the world, the Moors in Spain were teaching geography to their children, with brass globes.

Lambert.— *When they were ready to, etc.* Why did you halt or hesitate here? The venerable Bede taught the rotundity of the earth before your beloved Moors had established themselves in Spain. He was canonized. And Gerbert in the tenth century used a globe in teaching astronomy. The history of the Moors in Spain is the history of wars and bloodshed from the time they invaded that unhappy country till they were whipped out of it.

Ingersoll.— The Moors in Spain were teaching geography to their children, with brass globes.

Lambert.— And while the Moors were so occupied, the Christian missionaries and teachers were teaching literature, the classics and the sciences in the schools of Europe. It is not necessary to lose time and space in naming the educational establishments which laid the foundation of our present civilization. Any text-book of history will give you the information. But as you are fond of contrasts, we will draw another. You say these Moors, Berbers and Mohammedans were intellectually far beyond the Christians. Well, centuries have passed and Christian and Mohammedan influences have had full opportunity of development. The first has progressed till it has produced the highest civilization in the world in political liberty, literature, and the arts and sciences. The second retrograded till the Moors have become a tribe of wandering cut-throats on the northern coasts of Africa, whom Christian nations have had to punish for their piracies. Our own government had to teach them a lesson of good behavior with shot and shell. And the Mohammedans of Turkey and Arabia are reverting into barbarism. Where are the arts and sciences among them now? You have admitted that these people started out with greater advantages than Christians, plus brass globes and Mohammedanism, while the poor, ignorant cut-throat Christians started out with every disadvantage, plus Christianity. Compare the two civilizations and the countries under them to-day. Look on this picture and then on that.

Ingersoll.—It has been very poetically said by

Mrs. Browning that "science was thrust into the brain of Europe on the point of the Moorish lance."

Lambert.— It would have been of more consequence if it had been truthfully said. You are like Mopsa in "Winter's Tale:"—

"I love a ballad in Print, a'-life; for then we are sure they are true."

But what sciences did these Moors punch into our European heads with lances?

Ingersoll.— From the Arabs we got our numerals, making mathematics of the higher branches practical.

Lambert.— Baron Von Humboldt was not a poet like Mrs. Browning, but it will be conceded that he is a better authority in science and its history. This renowned scholar says: "The profound and important historical investigations to which a distinguished mathematician, M. Chasles, was led by his correct interpretation of the so-called Pythagorian table in the geometry of Boethius, render it more than probable that the Christians in the West were acquainted even earlier than the Arabians with the Indian system of enumeration; the use of the nine figures, having their value determined by position, being known by them under the name of the system of the Abacus." ("Cosmos," vol. ii., pages 226 and 358.)

Speaking of the so-called Arabic numerals, the Encyclopædia Britannica (art. arithmetic) says: "They are now generally acknowledged to be of Indian origin. . . . It was probably in the following century (that is, the eleventh) that the Arabs introduced the notation into Spain." Now it is known that Gerbert, Pope Sylvester II., taught these Indian numerals in the tenth century. I think the scientist Humboldt's authority is good enough to offset that of the poet. While on the question of mathematical science, we may draw another comparison between the condition of mathematical science in Mohammedan countries at the present time as compared with Christian countries.

Ingersoll.—We also got from them (the Arabs) the art of making cotton paper, which is almost at the foundation of modern intelligence.

Lambert.—Then why did they not continue to use that art and compete in the race of intelligence? Compare the intelligence of modern Christian Europe with that of Mohammedan Turkey, Egypt and Africa of to-day! Arabia lies between India, where paper was manufactured, and Southern Europe. The Mohammedans, among other of their prowling and robbing expeditions, took, in 702, Samarkand, where they learned to make cotton paper and introduced it into Europe. As cotton does not grow in Europe, owing to the climate, it is natural that European peoples would know nothing of its use until introduced by somebody, and it is also natural that the intervening nation should introduce it. We can see no argument against Christianity in this, as Christianity received no commission to teach people the use of the cotton plant. That was left to the enterprise of commerce. It is strange you have no suggestions to make to the founder of Christianity on the advantages of paper and calico. I am not aware that the Koran gives any instructions on the subject. But compare the use of that plant in Christian and Mohammedan countries at the present day, and what is the conclusion we must come to in reference to comparative enterprise and intelligence?

Ingersoll.— We learned from them to make cotton cloth, making cleanliness possible in Christendom.

Lambert.— What I have said about cotton paper applies equally to cotton cloth. It was an Indian invention, brought to the West through Arabia. Again I say, compare the use and manufacture of cotton cloth in Christian and Mohammedan countries to-day, and draw a conclusion. Soap is a more useful article in the way of cleanliness than cotton. What a pity you could not introduce it to filthy Christians on the point of a Moorish lance. As you are so fond of those Arabian Mohammedans, it is strange you would not prefer to live among them. But you know better. If you lived among them and talked against their religion and Koran as you talk against the religion and Bible of Christians, among whom you live in peace, they would bow-string you or tie you up in a sack and throw you into the Bosphorus, where no doubt you would float, buoyant as a gas bag.

Ingersoll.— It will not do to say that the religion of the Greeks was true because the Greeks were the greatest sculptors.

Lambert.— It is a great advantage to have a man among us who is able to clear up this obscure point with a dash of his pen. But who ever claimed it would "do to say" it? That is what I would like to know. I am not aware that the Greeks ever made such a claim, or that any one made it for them. Then why argue against a position that no one seems to know anything about?

Ingersoll.— Neither is it an argument in favor of monarchy that Shakespeare, the greatest of men, was born and lived in a monarchy.

Lambert.— Neither is it an argument against a republic that Ingersoll lives and talks gush, blasphemy and cheap learning in it. But it is an argument that a Christian people love liberty and will put up with abuse of it rather than abolish the use of it.

The works of Shakespeare are a proof of the beneficent influence of Christianity, for those masterpieces of thought are inexplicable if you take away the Christian truths and moral principles upon which the mighty fabrics of his genius are based. If Shakespeare's works were forgotten, and a thousand years hence a copy were found, the reader would know that their philosophy and motive are Christian. It fits only in Christian civilization and out of it is unintelligible. His genius was informed and directed by Christian thought. It is well to remember that this wonderful man was a Christian.

Ingersoll.— As a matter of fact the civilization of our time is the result of countless causes with which Christianity had little to do except by way of hindrance.

Lambert.— Then how account for the fact that the civilization of our times is found only where Christian influence and teaching prevail? There are four kinds of civilization — the Chinese, the Indian, the Mohammedan and the Christian, and the last is the civilization you refer to when you speak of "the civilization of our time." It is the result of the Christian idea of life and human destiny, spurring the human intellect to its highest activity and directing it to its highest development. Eliminate it from human affairs and the present state of enlightenment is inexplicable. Your dashing statement will not prevail against the great thinkers of modern times. Vigor of assertion does not supply the place of truth.

Ingersoll.— Does the Doctor think that the material progress of the world was caused by this passage: "Take no thought for the morrow?"

Lambert.— Speaking for myself, I should say that the material progress of the world is by no means the highest progress of the world. I believe that a Thomas of Aquin, a Michael Angelo, a Raphael, a Copernicus, a Galileo, a Kepler, a Dante, a Shakespeare, a Newton, a Descartes and a Leibnitz do more honor to humanity and express a higher progress and civilization than all your Girards and Astors, Vanderbilts and Goulds, Rothschilds and Rockefellers, syndicates and corporations in existence put together. Intellectual progress stands on a higher plane than mere material progress — than wheat deals, coal deals, petroleum deals and other deals by which the wealth of a nation is absorbed by the few to the detriment of the many. But as you believe that nothing but matter and its forms exist, your low groveling and gross idea of progress is a matter of course, as with your philosophy there can be no spiritual, moral or intellectual world. But even this material progress is the result of the higher, the intellectual progress and energy with which the genius of Christianity inspired those under its influence—for outside this Christian influence there is not even material progress. This material progress follows the light of Christianity as the waves of the ocean heave up and follow the light of the moon. It is needless to say that it is not because of any one text of Scripture or any one Christian law, and no one should ask such a foolish question. It is the result of Christianity as a unit of force and influence extending its energies in every field of human activity.

Ingersoll.— The Rev. Mr. Peters, in answer, takes the ground that the Bible has produced the richest and most varied literature the world has ever seen.

Lambert.— His ground is solid and invincible, as you would have seen if you had allowed your powerful mind to meditate long enough on it, to take in its full import. It is not too late yet. We will meditate on it together.

Ingersoll.— This, I think, is hardly true.

Lambert.— You think.

Ingersoll.— Has not most modern literature been produced in spite of the Bible?

Lambert.— Do you ask this question for information, or do you insinuate it as a sort of interrogative argument? But in any case I answer that most modern literature has not been produced in spite of the Bible, and I will go further and say it would not have been produced at all if the Bible and Christianity had not existed. But proceed.

Ingersoll.— Did not Christians, for many generations, take the ground that the Bible was the only important book?

Lambert.— No, they did not.

Ingersoll.— And that books differing from the Bible should be destroyed?

Lambert.— No, they did not. Having answered each question categorically I will now reply to the general drift of your interrogative argument — which is the lowest and most non-committal kind of reasoning known to logic. A system of religion, when its doctrines once take possession of a people's mind, develops itself in their individual, social, political, ethical and æsthetical life, and becomes the foundation of all these forms. To the æsthetical life belong literature, art and science. Hence it is that the books which contain the dogmas of a religious system are the foundation, the source from which are developed the habits of thought, the literature, arts and sciences of a people whose minds have been imbued with those dogmas of fundamental religious principles. The writings of Lao-tse and Confucius are the basis of Chinese social, political and ethical life, and the foundation of their art, science and literature. The Zend-Avesta of Zoroaster is the same for the Persians, the Vedas and the writings of Gautama Buddha for the East Indians, the Koran for the Mohammedans, and the Bible for the Jews and Christians. Now all these peoples have, during the course of ages worked out in their forms of life and thought those dogmas which once took possession of them. Hence the difference in their life, history, literature and art. Now as the writings of Confucius form the basis of Chinese literature and the Koran that of Mohammedan, so in like manner the Bible is the foundation of Christian literature. You will observe as the books differ the literature differs, and as Christian literature is the most excellent in the world — the fundamental religious principles which are found in the Bible are the most excellent and true. An apple-tree produces apples, a pear-tree pears, a peach-tree peaches — each according to the nature of the life that animates its roots. All these various civilizations and literatures are the fruits of the different religious systems. The founder of Christianity says: "By their fruits ye shall know them." By Christian literature I do not mean only books that have been written on Christian subjects or in defense of Christian doctrines, but the whole body of literature of whatever kind and character that is called Christian in contradistinction with Pagan, Chinese, Indian, Mohammedan literature, in a word, all that vast intellectual structure that has been built up in the Christian world and life during the last eighteen hundred years. And I say that the word of God is the source, foundation and centre of it all — the leaven in the dough. What! you will ask, is Shakespeare and Molière and Lope de Vega and all the works of fiction and history and art and sciences, Christian literature? I answer yes. They are all the result of that intellectual fermentation produced by the introduction of Christian revelation into human society, and the influence it threw around the human mind. Even the infidel cannot throw off the influence in which he is born and grows up, for his mind is like the chameleon; it takes its color from the food on which it feeds and the environments in which it lives. Hence, the thoughts, even of the infidel in the Christian pale, run parallel to or against Christianity. However he may try to avoid it, his thoughts move in reference to Christianity. He cannot think like a Chinese or a Hindoo. He must think in Christian modes of thought — even when he fights against it. It was probably thoughts like these that the Rev. Mr. Peters had in mind when he said that the Bible produced the richest and most varied literature in the world. But did not Christianity destroy books that differed from the Bible? Even granting this, it would not help your argument, for Rev. Mr. Peters referred to a literature that exists, not to a literature that is destroyed.

Ingersoll.— In short, the philosophy that enlightens and the fiction that enriches the brain, would not exist. The greatest literature the world has ever seen is, in my judgment, the poetic — the dramatic; that is to say, the literature of fiction in its widest sense would never have been published.

Lambert.—No one who reads your writings need be told that you are fond of fiction. But all this great literature you speak of was published in Christian times and countries. Dante, Alfieri, Metastasio, Goldoni, Silvio Pellico and others in Italy; Calderon, Cervantes, Lope de Vega, in Spain; Molière, Le Sage, Racine, in France; Spencer, Ben Jonson, Shakespeare, Beaumont, Fletcher, Milton,

Tennyson, and others in England, were Christians, and were applauded, encouraged and supported by Christians.

Ingersoll.— Certainly, if the Church could have had control, the plays of Shakespeare would never have been written.

Lambert.— Shakespeare lived and wrote under Elizabeth and James. Under these two monarchs the Church of England held full sway, and many were put to death on account of their religion; and I do not see why they could not have hanged or beheaded Shakespeare if they had so desired. But he lived, encouraged by monarchs and people, all of whom were Christians, and died in peace in the Christian faith, as the following extract from his last will and testament will show:—

"In the name of God, Amen. I, William Shakespeare, of Stratford-upon-Avon, in the county of Warwick, gent., in perfect health and memory, (God be praised!) do make and ordain in this my last will and testament in manner and form following; that is to say: First, I commend my soul into the hands of God my Creator, hoping and assuredly believing, through the only merits of Jesus Christ my Savior, to be made partaker of life everlasting; and my body to the earth, whereof it is made."

Such is the creed that gave direction to the mighty genius of the greatest poet that ever wrote. You have a lecture on Shakespeare, and no doubt studied him somewhat, besides what you ate to prepare it. You probably read his will, and yet you write: "If the Church could have had control, the plays of Shakespeare would never have existed." Is it honest?

Ingersoll.— Thousands of theological books have been written on thousands of questions of no possible importance. Libraries have been printed on subjects not worth discussing,— not worth thinking about,— and that will, in a few years, be regarded as puerile by the whole world.

Lambert.— There is no doubt of it. You have written some works on Moses and other scripture subjects. A great many useless books have been printed and are being printed, which time has relegated and will relegate to trunk makers. But the fact still remains that Christians were the founders of the great libraries where books on science, history, philosophy, theology, classics and the drama, were preserved with care. This fact alone is enough to disprove your oft-repeated assertion that Christianity is the enemy of learning, for had it been it would have imitated your beloved Turks who destroyed the great Alexandrian library. The argument of the Mohammedan leader in justification of his act of vandalism was that if that celebrated library contained more than the Koran, it contained too much and should be destroyed. If it contained the same, it was unnecessary and should be destroyed; and if it contained less, it was insufficient and should be destroyed. So it was to be destroyed in any case. It is unnecessary to say that Christianity never adopted this destructive logic.

Ingersoll.— The best modern historians of whom I have any knowledge are Voltaire, Hume, Gibbon, Buckle and Draper.

Lambert.— Your admiration is accounted for when we know that all these writers are anti-Christians. But to show the value of your judgment of the character of historians, I will give the opinions of some men whose judgment will be considered of more weight than yours. And first as to Voltaire, as you mention him first.

Frederick Schlegel writes: " Whilst French literature was stocked with the productions of l ly narrators, couched in respectable and easy diction, it was altogether without a really classic national history, the work of some great original genius. Of this want, then, Voltaire was fully cognizant, and, in accordance with the comprehensive grasp of his ambition, he sought to supply that want.

France herself acknowledged the utter failure of his attempt; and that neither in point of art nor of representation and style, suited to the range of history, can he for a moment be compared, I will not say with the best ancient authors, but with the leading historians of England."

Mathews in his "Hours with Men and Books" says: "The man who has not a high ideal of the historian's office, can never achieve success as one." "History," wrote Voltaire to a friend, "is, after all, nothing but a parcel of tricks we play with the dead. As for the portraits of men, they are nearly all the creatures of fancy; 'tis a monstrous piece of charlatanry to pretend to paint a personage with whom you have never lived." Lecky, himself a rationalist, in his "Rationalism in Europe," says that Voltaire has a deep stain upon his memory— "A dark, damning stain which all his services can never efface: He applauded the partition of Poland."

You probably never read "Letters of Certain Jews to Voltaire," in which he is proved to be as untrustworthy in his statements about the Bible as even yourself.

You next mention Hume as one of the best modern historians.

Of this historian, Lecky says: "Whilst Bishop

Horsley was proclaiming that subjects had nothing to say to the laws except to obey them, Hume was employing all his skill in investing with the most seductive colors the policy of the Stuarts, in rendering the great supporters of liberty in the seventeenth century odious or ridiculous, and in throwing into the most plausible aspects the maxims of their opponents."

Of this same Hume, Schlegel wrote: "He can only be regarded as an eminent party historian, the first in his peculiar method and view, not the truly great author of a performance at once natural in spirit and in genius. His description of earlier times is very unsatisfactory; having no affection for them he could not sufficiently realize them."

"It was," says Mathews, "a favorite boast of his (Hume's) that his first account of the Stuarts was free from all bias and that he had held the balance between Whig and Tory with a delicate, impartial hand. Ten years after the first publication of his work, irritated by the outcry against him 'for presuming,' as he expressed it, ' to shed a generous tear for the fate of Charles I. and the Earl of Stafford,' he avenged the censure *by recasting his historical verdicts, so as to render them offensive to the party that attacked him* . . . Hume changed the description of Mary's character, in his history, because his printer said he would lose five hundred pounds by the publication of it. 'Indeed,' said Hume, 'he almost refused to print it; so I was obliged to alter it as you saw.' . . . We need not be surprised, therefore, that the searching investigation, to which his history was subjected some years ago by George Brodie, brought to light so many departures from truth both wilful and intentional."

Cobbet's opinion of Hume is given in his usual vigorous style. He describes his " certain, unquestioned facts " as " a tissue of malignant lies " and speaks of " the malignity of this liar " who was " a great, fat fellow, fed in considerable part out of *public money*, without having merited it by any real public service."

Coleridge in his " Biographia Literaria " accuses Hume of having stolen bodily his famous " Essay on Association " from the Commentary of St. Thomas Aquinas on the " Parva Naturalia " of Aristotle.

Macaulay says : " Hume is an accomplished advocate. Without positively asserting much more than he can prove, he gives prominence to all the circumstances which support his case; he glides lightly over those which are unfavorable to it; his own witnesses are applauded and encouraged: the statements which seem to throw discredit on them are controverted; the contradictions into which they fall are explained away; a clear and connected abstract of their evidence is given. Everything that is offered on the other side is scrutinized with the utmost severity; every suspicious circumstance is a ground for comment and invective; what cannot be denied is extenuated or passed by without notice; *concessions even are sometimes made; but this insidious candor only increases the effect of the vast mass of sophistry.*" "The same author," says Gibbon, "deserves very severe censure on the same ground."

Professor Adamson in the "Encyclopædia Britannica," says of Hume's "History of England:" "It has been the business of subsequent historians to correct his misrepresentations so far as they referred to the period of which he had fair knowledge, and to supersede his accounts of those periods which his insufficiency of knowledge disabled him from treating in a manner worthy of him. The early portion of his *history* may be regarded as now of little value."

As to Gibbon, the author of "Hours with Men and Books," writes: "The author of 'The Decline and Fall of the Roman Empire' has *Gibbonized* the vast tract over which he has traversed. The qualities of the historian's character steal out in every paragraph; and the reader who is magnetized by his genius rises from the perusal of the vast work informed of nothing as it was in itself, but of everything as it appeared to Gibbon, and especially doubting two things — *that there is any chastity in women or any divine truth in Christianity.*"

Macaulay says of Gibbon : " He writes like a man who had received some personal injury from Christianity, and wished to be revenged on it and all its professors."

And Whately says of Gibbon: "His way of writing reminds one of those persons who never dare look you in the face."

As to the other two whom you mention, Buckle and Draper, I know little, but as you put them in your list I deem that alone sufficient reason to conclude that they are of the same kidney as the others.

There, Mr. Ingersoll, are the men you name as the best modern historians. Of course, you qualify your statement by saying "of whom I have any knowledge —" which is a very important qualification indeed.

Ingersoll.— The gentleman (Dr. Peters) makes another mistake, and a very common one.

Lambert.— The gentleman made no mistake. He struck the true key to reply to you. You had stated that "the Church was an enemy of education." He, to show the untruthfulness of this, adduced an overwhelming array of evidence. What did you do? Did you meet him fair and square like an honest, candid man and withdraw your accusation or attempt to discredit the facts adduced by him? No; you sneaked away from the defense of your charge and pretended that his facts were adduced to prove the divine origin of Christianity — a point that was not then in question. You are an eely opponent, and one needs to have sand in one's hand to hold you. You constructed a little abortion of a syllogism and attributed it to him thus: —

Ingersoll.— This is his (Dr. Peter's) argument: Christian countries are the most intelligent; therefore they owe that intelligence to Christianity. Then the next step is taken. Christianity being the best, having produced these results, must have been of divine origin.

Lambert.—Dr. Peters made no such argument in his reply to you and when you say he did you show an utter want of that candor of which you talk so much. He adduced facts to disprove your false statement that "the Church is an enemy of education," and the divine origin of Christianity came not in the line of his reasoning. Just here is the irksomeness of disputing with you. One must be eternally correcting your blunders and misrepresentations and holding you to keep you from dodging issues after you have raised them. There is nothing easier than putting silly arguments in the mouth of your opponent and then displaying your dexterity in oversetting them. It is a little game of this kind that I have caught you in here. No Christian with any logic in his head argues that, because Christian civilization is the highest and best in the world that the Christian religion is therefore of divine origin. As well might one argue that Howe's sewing machine is superior to all others; therefore Howe's sewing machine is of divine origin. And thus you dodge your opponent's fact by misrepresenting him and Christians, and then go off with a lot of unmitigated rot about Egypt and Rome, Greece and India. I will show you how the Christian argues and see what you can make of it. Christian civilization is superior to any other civilization in the world. Christian civilization is the result of Christian principles, from which it springs. Therefore Christian principles are superior to the principles underlying any other civilization. You will observe that the purpose here is not to prove the divine origin of Christianity, but the superiority of its principles or fundamental truths, over those of all other religions of the world. Having got this far, the mind is prepared to consider the arguments for the divine origin of the religion which teaches those truths. How different this sounds from your tricky presentation of an argument, which enabled you to ring in your familiar pagan roundelay.

Ingersoll.—Is it not evident to all that if the churches in Europe had been institutions of learning—

Lambert.—The churches were the centres around which the institutions of learning, the schools and universities clustered.

Ingersoll.—If the domes of cathedrals had been observatories—

Lambert.—I am not aware that it was forbidden to make observations from these domes. The tower of Pisa is attached to the Cathedral, and it was good enough for Galileo.

Ingersoll.—If the priests had been teachers of the facts of nature, the world would have been far in advance of what it is to-day.

Lambert.—In other words, if the ninth century had been the nineteenth, this would be the twenty-ninth century.

Ingersoll.—Countries depend on something besides their religion for progress.

Lambert.—This is one of those profound observations of yours that make your admirers stare in wonder. I venture to say you will find nothing like it in any philosophy from Plato and Aristotle down to Guilielmus Prope, more commonly known as Bill Nye. I am sure I never read anything quite up to it, and I hope I never will. It has such a titillating effect on the risible muscles when it comes on one with an honestly-believe-honor-bright-courage-of-the-soul sort of suddenness. I frankly admit its truth, and all the more readily as I have so rarely the opportunity of agreeing with you. Without food and drink enough to keep body and soul together, progress, at least in this world, would be of a rather jejune character. But the progress produced by food and drink without fundamental truths enough to give the human mind a good working majority would be of a fat and lumpish kind; while the indispensable conditions of life, plus true religion, give true civilization and progress.

Ingersoll.— Nations with a good soil can get along quite well with an exceedingly poor religion.

Lambert.— Egypt has the most fruitful soil in the world. Yearly the Nile feeds it with its rich, fruit-bearing deposits, so that it needs but the touch of the human hand to make it smile with waving golden grain. Notwithstanding all this, it does not seem to have got on quite well with an exceedingly poor religion. Turkey is a good soil and so is India, Persia and Africa; they have exceedingly poor religions there, yet they don't seem to have got on quite well, particularly as compared with less favored countries where they have the true — that is the Christian — religion. While the latter are alive, flourishing, intelligent and civilized, the former seem to suffer under an intellectual blight that paralyzes energy and produces stagnation. During your profound meditation did this contrast ever occur to your powerful mind? True, they got on, but they do not get on "quite well," as a doctor would tell you after examining their condition, though he might assure you with professional confidence that they are getting on "as well as could be expected under the circumstances."

Ingersoll.— And no religion has yet been good enough to give wealth and happiness to human beings when climate and soil were bad and barren.

Lambert.— This is another of your sage remarks. But I am not aware that any one ever recommended religion as a substitute for climate and soil, and if you imagine that religion was introduced into the world as a sort of guano bed plus a moral code you have been laboring under a false impression. Did it ever occur to you that in those parts of the world where nature is most generous of her gifts and bestows them on man with lavish profusion, religion has but little influence and the arts and sciences are unknown? Follow the equator with the sun around the globe and you will observe this striking fact.

Ingersoll.— Religion supports nobody.

Lambert.— The "American Cyclopædia," in supplement to volume 9, tells us that your father was a Congregational minister. As a rule, ministers and their families are supported by their congregations on the Pauline principle — that he who serves at the altar should live by the altar. There was a time, then, when the bread you ate, the bed you slept on, and even the little baggy, blue jean breeches you wore were supplied from the penny collection and the clergyman's salary. You err, then, when you say, with such dogmatic fervor, that "religion supports nobody." It is in this sense only that religion is a "perpetual mendicant" — as you so elegantly express it. Applause has weakened your memory, and made you forget that in your cynical and cruel words you were branding your parents as agents of religion in its perpetual mendicant business, and, like Ham, ridiculing your own father's nakedness. I do not say you did this unfilial thing intentionally, you simply did not think of it. I do not speak of these things, which your coarse remark has forced me to refer to, as a humiliation or dishonor. The dishonor and disgrace is in the forgetting of it, and the gross ingratitude of it, and your mean fling at religion as a "mendicant," in your pride of success and better circumstances. How embarrassed you would be to introduce the honest old Congregational minister and his wife to your present following! And how embarrassed those old folks would be, and how sorrowful! It is well they sleep in peaceful and honored graves. They suffer no pain or shame from the coarse diatribes of their unworthy son against the religion that cheered their weary way through life and gave them hope of peace and rest beyond. You mention with pride the name of Franklin. Let me quote for your benefit from a letter he wrote to Paine to dissuade him from publishing his infamous "Age of Reason." It runs thus: "Among us it is not necessary, as among Hottentots, that a youth to be raised into the company of men should prove his manhood by beating his mother."

In these remarks some of your kid-gloved, eiderdown namby-pambies may accuse me of harshness.

I ask them what they think — if they can perform that operation — of your expression that "religion is a perpetual mendicant. It lives on the labor of others, and then has the arrogance to pretend that it supports the giver," and your saying in reference to Christian ministers in relation to Voltaire's death: "Upon the fences of expectation gathered the unclean birds of superstition impatiently awaiting their prey." Has a man who talks in this way a right to be treated with any reference to his supposed delicate feelings? I believe in dealing with men like you we should not lose time or space in concocting fine-spun, delicate turns of expression to cover up or soften the thoughts suggested by your conduct and your sophistries and misrepresentations. Your fancy phrases and rounding periods do not make your coarse insults any the less offensive and outrageous; and those intellectually flabby people who imagine you should be always touched with lavender kids are the best illustrations of Darwin's theory of man's descent from those burlesque imitations of him — the gibbering, grinning, lascivious, unclean, vile-smelling monkeys. They are standing evidences of an unwholesome and perverted taste. It is always proper to call a spade a spade. I cannot understand how some men calling themselves ministers of Christ, and wishing to be considered as such, and drawing their pay as such, and wearing long-tailed coats and white neckties as such, can phrase their replies to your insults to their creed and Creator as if they courted the sunshine of your fat smile of approval, fished for compliments at your hands, and wished to be considered by you as fine, liberal, broad-minded fellows, wonderfully out of place in the pulpit. They would honor religion more by stepping down out of their pulpits, and openly and at once enrolling themselves under your flag. It is a small compliment to you to say I respect you more than I do them. Their conduct is the saddest commentary on the times we live in, and they deserve the loaded lash of the whip with which you have so frequently scourged them. I think if there could be a plea made for the mitigation of the sentence of Judas Iscariot, it should be said of him that while he betrayed his best friend and master, he did not wear a white choker or a pious simper and pretend to be His friend after he had kissed Him; and that he quit the ministry and hanged himself with a halter, thus ridding the world of the scandal of his visible continuance. I believe on the great day of reckoning, in the Valley of Decision, the Judge of the quick and the dead will look on you and Judas Iscariot with less disapprobation and loathing than on those panderers to your inordinate vanity.

You are a child of Christendom. This fact is beyond your power to change. You are a prodigal, it is true. But when old age makes the quick blood move slowly, when the pleasures that please lose their charm and become husks and Dead Sea apples,— stale and unprofitable,— when your mind, free from the pressure of excitement incident to ephemeral applause, settles down to think of the problem of human life and destiny in a manner and with the mental integrity worthy of it, you may come back again weary and heart-sick of all shams and rejoice those whom you now scandalize. This is a possible but not a probable ending of the agnostic scene when the curtain falls and shuts from your sight forever the bright world which you have made the god of your idolatry. Death points its skeleton finger at us all, and when the light of eternity begins to shine in our faces, the honest man is strong enough to try to put himself right with the universe and square his mind to the truth.

CHAPTER VI.

Ingersoll.— Neither can I admit that Christianity abolished slavery.

Lambert.— There were twenty millions of slaves in the Roman Empire at the advent of Christianity. They were freed by Christian teaching and legislation. To prove this I will give the names of some councils which legislated to protect the slave: The council of Elvira in the year 305; the council of St. Patrick held in Ireland in 450 required church property to be used in redeeming captives. The council of Agde in 506; the council of Epaon in 517; the fifth council of Arles in 549; third council of Lyons in 583; second of Macon in 585; third of Toledo in 589; fifth of Paris in 614; Rheims in 625; fourth of Toledo in 633; Emerita in 666; eleventh of Toledo in 675; another of Toledo in 694; the second of Verneuil which also required church property to be used in redeeming captives; the council of Worms in 868. A council held in 922 declared that he who sold another into slavery was guilty of homicide. A council held in London in 1102 forbade the selling of men in that city, and called it an infamous traffic. The second council of Lyons excommunicated those who enslaved others. Pope Gregory XVI. in 1839

I.C.S.—11

published apostolic letters against the slave trade. I might mention many other councils, but I have given enough to show the spirit and tendency of Christianity on the subject of slavery and that anti-slavery is a Christian thought. You will seek in vain for it in the writings of the great Greek and Roman philosophers. Yet you tell us you cannot admit that Christianity abolished slavery and that the church exerted itself against slavery! At the advent of Christianity slavery existed in all countries now in the pale of Christendom. Within that pale it exists no longer, while beyond that pale it exists still. This fact of itself is sufficient to prove that the spirit of Christianity is inimical to slavery.

Ingersoll.—Many of the abolitionists were infidels.

Lambert.—Some infidels may have talked about abolitionism as they are always ready to do about anything, but it was the Christian people with muskets in their hands that nerved Lincoln to write the Proclamation. I never heard of any infidel regiments or brigades in the war—that awkward squad can always be found in the rear—talking. One of their strong points is what John Chinaman in his Pigeon English calls *talkee, talkee*. But I must admit, Colonel, you did go to the front to man the deadly breach. Mr. Redpath, an admirer of your wit, gives, in illustration of it, an incident in your brilliant military career. The rebels, it appears, chased you into a corner, when you offered to acknowledge the blanked confederacy if they would stop their blankety-blanked shooting. So you were taken prisoner and General Forest, a caustic humorist and a good soldier, showed his appreciation of you by expressing a willingness to exchange you for a mule! Redpath does not inform us under what cartel you were exchanged, or what became of the mule, but when they let you go it appears you went home, leaving your comrades in arms nothing but your invaluable example to console them for your loss. With your notions of life and death, one cannot blame you for avoiding the dangers of promiscuous shooting. If this life is all you have, you should take good care of it. It is what the timorous little rabbit does, and instinct is a great thing. But if your comrades had had the same "courage of the soul," the South would have had a picnic of it, that is, if they did not take the notion to stampede us all over the Canadian line. Luckily those comrades were inspired neither by your courage nor your philosophy. But few skipped from the ranks to their safe homes. The great majority remained until union, freedom and peace were secured. Your short and brilliant military career taught you, as one of the "results of the human mind," that soldiering in the South was neither as safe nor lucrative as blackguarding the Christian religion in the North; so bravely turning your back on the dangers of the battlefield, you boldly faced the dangers of the lecture hall, and with reckless courage charged on the gods, myths and miracles, and on Moses, when you knew he was dead long enough not to be dangerous.

It is well for the country and for the cause of freedom that our brave men who languished and died in Southern prisons were not of such accommodating stuff. It is amusing to hear your injudicious admirer alluding to this incident in your short military career as a proof that you are a "fellow of infinite jest." He seems not to have seen that he exhibited you as a cowardly poltroon who later on in the war would have been court-martialed and shot. You are not afraid of Almighty God; bless you, no, but a loaded musket with the glittering eye of a Confederate at the further end of it is quite another thing. It is enough to make one sick, and requires great "courage of the soul" to look at it. Had the manly men of the North been equally "brave" the clank of the chain would still mingle with the groans of the slave.

It required men like Grant, Sherman and Sheridan, who feared God and not the musket, to put down the rebellion and give freedom to the slave. And now, when these ends have been attained, the talkative infidel is once more to the front — ready to advise and instruct everybody in general and the Almighty in particular.

Slavery is not yet abolished throughout the world. The traffic in slaves still exists in Africa, notwithstanding the efforts of Christian nations to abolish it. Cardinal Levigerie is at the head of a society of monks who devote their lives to destroy the slave traffic. His headquarters are in Algiers. A pathetic incident at the inauguration of the movement is worth telling. They had rescued a little slave girl whose hand had been cruelly cut off by her Mohammedan owners. The stump was still bleeding and the amputated hand was secured. The Cardinal introduced this little child to the assemblage some time after and, while exhorting his followers to their work, he raised the poor little dead and shrivelled hand in his and pointing it to the southward, said: "Comrades, this hand shall be our emblem and point out for us the direction of our duty, and be to us a constant reminder of it." There is no agnostic wishy-washy about this great Christian philanthropist.

Ingersoll.— Mr. Peters says: "Why is it that in Christian countries you find the greatest amount of physical and intellectual liberty, the greatest freedom of thought, speech and action?" Is this true of all?

Lambert.— Yes, sir, it is true of all as compared to non-Christian nations, and that is the comparison implied in Rev. Mr. Peter's question. Compare any Christian nation with non-Christian nations of the world and you will see the almost incredible superiority of the former over the latter in intelligence, freedom, progress, prosperity and civilization. But that is precisely the comparison you wish to avoid.

Ingersoll.— How about Spain and Portugal?

Lambert.— Well compare Spain and Portugal with Egypt, Turkey, Persia, India, and you will see that they are all right.

Mentioning Spain reminds me that it was Spain, through her minister d'Urquija, that enabled Humboldt to make his explorations in the New World. It was his observations on this expedition that enabled him to lay the foundations of the science of physical geography and meteorology, and to Spain we owe the result of his labors, as to the same country we owe the discovery of the Western Continent.

Ingersoll.—There is more infidelity in France than in Spain.

Lambert.—And more immorality. Infidels once had control for a short time in France and they showed their animus. That short period in the history of France is called, by common consent, the *Reign of Terror*.

Ingersoll.—There is far more infidelity in England than there was a century ago, and there is far more liberty than there was a century ago.

Lambert.—The liberty of England is the outgrowth of her constitution and Magna Charta, and both these reach far back into Christian times when modern infidelity was unknown. Those that gather the harvest must not for that reason boast of sowing the seed. The loquacious infidel is on the car of progress like the fly on the chariot wheel, "O, my, what a dust we make." Or he may be compared to the English sparrow, noisy, pugnacious, garrulous, useless and a nuisance, appropriating to himself the fruits of the laborers who sowed the seed of progress and civilization in silence and industry ages ago.

Ingersoll.—There is far more infidelity in England than there was a century ago.

Lambert.—And more rascality, more immorality, more penitentiaries, jails and lunatic asylums.

Your purpose was to make the progress of liberty commensurate with that of infidelity, and then imply that the former is the result of the latter. But the sophism is easily exposed by an illustration. There is more misery, want, wretchedness and general hopelessness among the common people of England than there was a century ago, and you tell us that there is more infidelity. Are you prepared to infer that the former is the result of the latter? If not, you must not insinuate that English liberty of to-day is the result of infidelity.

Ingersoll.— There is far more infidelity in the United States than there was fifty years ago, and a hundred infidels to-day where there was one fifty years ago.

Lambert.— There is far more rascality, thieving, fraud, murders, suicide, divorces, immorality, jails, penitentiaries, houses of correction, lunatic asylums, vagrants, tramps and general "cussedness" than there was fifty years ago. And we begin to see the cause of it when you tell us that there are one hundred infidels now where there was one fifty years ago. There appears to be a "concatenation accordingly."

Ingersoll.— Mr. Ballou insists that God has the same right to punish us that nature has, or that the state has. I do not think he understands what

I have said. The state ought not to punish for the sake of punishment.

Lambert.— Mr. Ballou did not make the right of the Supreme Being to punish us dependent on the right of the state to punish us. He is evidently too clear-headed a theologian and logician for that. As a theologian he knows that there are no rights of any kind whatever in existence that are not immediately or remotely derived from the Supreme Being. And as a logician he knows that to prove a greater right by the fact of a lesser one would be inconclusive. He knows the law of logic that the conclusion must be contained in the premises, and that the finite right of a finite state, taken as a premise, does not include the infinite right of the Infinite Being. The argument runs in the opposite direction, for from the infinite right of the Supreme Being we derive the right of the state to punish us when we deserve it. In this the Christian is logical and consistent.

Mr. Ballou's argument was of that kind known as *ad hominem*, an argument *at you*, and based on a concession which he knew you would make as a lawyer, namely, that a just state has the right to punish to the extent it judges sufficient to vindicate the outraged majesty of the laws and protect the welfare of its members. On this position, assumed rightly to be granted by you, he proceeds and asks, has not God, for a stronger reason (because the Author of the state and its rights) the right to inflict punishment on the guilty to the extent He deems necessary to vindicate the outraged majesty of His law and for the welfare of His creatures? It seems to me that this line of reasoning will stand the test of the severest logical criticism.

Ingersoll.— The state ought not to punish for the sake of punishment.

Lambert.— Who ever said it ought? Or that the Supreme Being ought, or does, or will punish for the *sake of* punishment?

Ingersoll.— The state may imprison or inflict what it calls punishment, first, for its own protection, and secondly, for the reformation of the punished.

Lambert.—This, then, is your position, and I propose to show that it is inconsistent with other doctrines taught by you. You are fond of inventing makeshift principles to meet particular exigencies, and then, when the occasion is past, forgetting them and teaching the very opposite. I will show now that your present doctrine is a good illustration of this.

All external human actions are the result of

thought — judgments and volitions externalized. You say: "Man is a machine, into which we put what we call food and produce what we call thought." And this process you call a "wonderful chemistry." Now, in view of this doctrine, I ask how you can consistently admit in the state the right to punish a man for committing an act which you call crime — for instance, killing his neighbor with malice aforethought? Surely if man is a machine, and his thoughts and acts depend on physiological and chemical laws, over which he has no control, he cannot be held as *guilty* of those acts, whatever they may be. His very malice aforethought is the food he ate before, digested and chemicised into thought and volition. What right, then, has the state to punish him for a murder which was only another form of food? for a murder which he could not avoid committing? The state in inflicting punishment supposes the existence of guilt. But there can be no guilt where there is no free agency, and therefore the man not being guilty cannot be punished by the state, any more than the state has a right to punish a locomotive that kills a man at a crossing, or a horse that kicks the brains out of its owner.

And suppose in spite of your man-machine doctrine the state determines to punish; for what will it punish him? Would it punish him for eating the food or for the act produced by the food independently of him? But why punish him for eating the murder-food when that very eating was the result of something he ate before, and that the result of something before, till we trace him down and find him clinging to his mother's breast. Was she the guilty party? If so we must trace her down.

You will now see how blindly inconsistent you are when you grant the state the right to punish, in order to make out a point against your opponent. But another thought suggests itself — the result perhaps of something I ate at dinner. It is this. The state is an aggregate of individual man-machines or human alembics, all busy digesting or spinning food into thought, as the spider spins his into web and the silkworm his into silk. Now I ask you where or how did this mass of busy machines acquire the right to punish anybody for anything? Is it the food they eat that generates in them the idea of punishment? If not, whence comes the idea, or the idea of guilt and innocence? And yet you tell us they have the right, "for the reformation of the punished." But this is no reason at all, for the reformation of the punished does not depend on punishment but on what he eats — that is, if your philosophy be true. If it prove anything, it only proves that the state has the right to *diet* him. Then it will have the difficult question to determine: What food produces innocence, and what guilt? It is irksome to argue against so fatuous a philosophy.

Lest you may try to twist yourself out of these results of your teachings, I will take the time and space to repeat another of your eloquent outpourings of concentrated unwisdom and inconsistency. Please repeat your doctrine of fatalism as found in "The Gods," page 55.

Ingersoll.— In the phenomena of mind we find the same endless chain of efficient causes; the same *mechanical* necessity . . . Every motive, every desire, every fear, hope and dream must have been *necessarily* produced. The facts and forces governing thought are as *absolute* as those governing the motions of the planets.

Lambert.— What I have said of your man-machine theory is equally, or with still greater force, applicable to the system of fatalism which you have here announced. While holding such doctrines I cannot see how you can have the "courage of the soul" to talk about rights of any kind, of states or individuals, or of guilt or innocence, vice or virtue, good or evil, liberty or slavery; or even of Christianity, itself, for, according to you, all these are but links in the endless chain, but various phases and evolutions of matter as it works out its activities from nowhere as a beginning to "the voiceless dust" as an end. Why declaim against Christianity since you must hold that it and all of what you call its crimes and iniquities are but a necessary phase of thoughtless nature. Why cry out against that nature which you tell us is "neither merciful nor cruel?" Why not imitate the silly cur and bay yourself hoarse at the moon?

Ingersoll.— If no one could do the state any injury, certainly the state would have no right to punish under the plea of protection.

Lambert.— Here there is a subtle sophism lurking under the word "injury." Certainly, if no one could do any injury to the state, the state could not punish for any injury done to it. But as a matter of fact any one can do injury to the state — not by upsetting or destroying it, mind — but by wounding the majesty of its authority, by contradicting its will as expressed in its laws, by bringing it into contempt, and by ill-treating its citizens or subjects.

In all these ways man can injure the state, and in the same ways he can injure the Supreme Being. He can disturb the harmony of the moral order and create discord and confusion, as a malicious musician in a grand orchestra can, by playing false notes, destroy the waves of melody and render the whole effect discordant and grating to the ear. The master of the orchestra would promptly eject him and take no further interest in him providing he kept out of there. God's providence is the music of the spheres, and while He has infinite patience with the defective, the weak and the incompetent, He has no tolerance for the malicious disturber of the harmony of the moral universe. Him He ejects — not for his bad playing but for his evil intent for which he, being a free agent, is personally responsible. Now, with this word "injury," cleared of its sophistical double sense, your argument based on it ceases to have any force.

Ingersoll.— And if no human being could by any possibility be reformed, then the excuse of reformation could not be given.

Lambert.—In the mind of the state, when it imprisons a criminal his reformation is the last consideration. He was put in to vindicate the majesty of authority and law, and that is done equally well whether the criminal reform or not. It removes a nuisance and a danger to society and thinks little further about it, just as a man will have a cancered hand removed and cast aside to prevent the other members from being equally affected. It is the duty of the state to see that the punishment is inflicted, that the criminal does not escape, and that no obstacle is placed in the way of his reformation. Further than this it need not go. The state is not a missionary to criminals. It appears that when a man commits a crime and is punished, you have no eyes for anybody else.

You present only two motives to justify punishment of criminals; the protection of the state from "injury" and the reformation of the criminal. Now, while the criminal may not be able to injure the state in the sense of destroying it, and while he is supposed to be irreformable, I have shown that there are still other reasons which justify and make it necessary to punish him, namely the vindication of authority, law and order, the protection of citizens and the prevention of law breaking by others who are held in restraint by the example of his just punishment,— others on whom love of goodness and rectitude and the moral law have little hold. Here we find reasons enough after eliminating the two of which you speak. These points being straightened out, we may proceed.

Ingersoll.— Let us apply this: If God be infinite,

no one can injure Him. Therefore He need not punish anybody or damn anybody or burn anybody for His protection.

Lambert.—*Injure Him!* The reader will please notice how the snakey little word "injure" is again introduced, and will remember what I said in beginning these articles, that in almost every sentence of yours there is a dead fly of sophistry that makes a scrutinizing and perhaps tedious analysis necessary — a sifting of the sodden mass to let air in. You may now repeat the major of your enthymeme.

Ingersoll.— If God be infinite, no one can injure Him.

Lambert.— God is infinite in every perfection, and the origin and source of all reality and all perfection known and unknown to the human mind, but it does not follow that no one can injure Him. No one, of course, can limit His power or destroy His existence, or in any way affect His personality; but every creature of His that He has ennobled by the gifts of intelligence and free will can injure Him, can insult His infinite majesty and disobey His law, can put His finite will in opposition to His infinite will, can defy Him and lower Him in the esteem of His intelligent creatures, can lie about and misrepresent Him, mislead His creatures for a time — but always with the understanding that He will one day vindicate His majesty, authority and law, so that the whole universe will know that He is a God who cannot be "injured" with impunity, even if to do so He must consign the evil doer, the evil-minded free agent, to eternal banishment from His presence, which is another way of saying hell. He will show in His own appointed time that a free agent in this phase of existence can place a cause that will have eternal consequences of good or ill, of happiness or misery.

You will please observe that the Supreme Being does not punish to "protect" Himself, but that His eternal justice and the ultimate equation of things make it necessary.

Ingersoll.— Let us take another step,—

Lambert.— By all means. Your steps thus far taken have not advanced you to any great extent.

Ingersoll.— Let us take another step. Punishment being justified only on two grounds,—

Lambert.— Allow me to interrupt you. It was only you who justified punishment *only on two grounds*. We have seen that there are several other grounds to justify it, which it was convenient for the nature of your argument to overlook, or forget, or at least not to mention. The whole force of your reasoning depended on there being *but two grounds*, whereas *there are several others.* You are logician enough to see that these *several other grounds* are fatal to your argument, and leave it like a punctured balloon to collapse and descend. You will now see why I was careful to bring into clear light the *other grounds.*

Ingersoll.— Punishment being justified only on two grounds,— that is, the protection of society and the reformation of the punished,— how can eternal punishment be justified?

Lambert.— In my mind's eye I can see your interrogative attitude and smile of triumph, but in as much as your exploded syllogistic process has lost the necessary buoyancy to float, we may leave it to be picked up and carted away for repairs. But, in spite of this, the question with which you finish your reasoning deserves calm consideration, not particularly for your sake, but for that of those who are blinded and dazzled by your sky-rocket sophistry.

How can eternal punishment be justified? On this question I meditate thus: The "results of the human mind" in the science of physics tell us that the raising of the hand, the flip of a butterfly's wing, the melody of the Jersey gallinipper or the hum of the busy bee produces a result in the Universe that changes the whole order of material things and changes them forever,— on the hypothesis that matter exists forever,— so that in all eternity things will never be as they were before. This is a truth of physical science. Now, as this is a truth of science in the world of matter, why is it not equally true in the world of mind or the moral world. Indeed, according to your own doctrine of materialism it *must* be true, for if there be nothing but matter and its potential forms, and matter is eternal; mind, intellect, soul, consciousness, being but matter in some of its forms, must be equally eternal. Then, if the flip of a butterfly's wing be eternal in its consequences, why is not the action of the intellect or soul in this or that direction also eternal in its consequences? Thus, you see science — not to speak of the Bible at all — teaches the eternity of good and evil consequences, heaven and hell, and as you do not allow God to interfere in the eternal laws of things you leave Him unable to free the soul from the eternal consequences of its acts, while, at the same time, you accused Him of cruelty for not doing so. Are you not just a little bit unreasonable?

Ingersoll.— Let us take another step. If instead of punishment we say "consequences" and that every good man has a right to reap the consequences of his good actions, and every bad man must bear the consequences of bad actions, then you must say to the good: If you stop doing good, you will lose the harvest. You must say to the bad: If you stop doing bad, you need not increase your burdens.

Lambert.— This is strange language for you to use after having taught, as we have seen above, that man's thoughts, desires, hopes and fears are the result of unalterable laws, over which he has no control, and that his thoughts, desires, etc., are links in the endless chain of resistless fate. If a man be doomed to suffer by laws over which he has no control, what difference does it make to him whether you call his misery a punishment or a consequence? Is it any consolation to the criminal to know that his hanging is not a punishment at all, but only a consequence? And if suffering reaches into the next world, as it must, according to the scientific facts noted above, what difference does it make to the sufferer whether it is called a punishment or a consequence? To him it certainly amounts to the same.

You say to the good man: *If you stop doing good, you will lose the harvest.* But why reason thus with him, after telling him that his every thought and action is determined by laws independent of him? Why treat him as a fool and play with him in this way? If he believes your doctrine of fate, he knows that to continue or stop doing good is not for him to determine, that his act can be neither good nor bad so far as he, a helpless victim of fate, is concerned; that whether he feeds the hungry or cuts a throat, his action is not his, but the mere unavoidable result of a law that is above and beyond his control, and that whatever comes to him, pain or pleasure cannot, by a free volition of his, be sought or avoided.

You say to the bad man: *If you stop doing bad, you need not increase your burdens.* But the bad man will quote your own philosophy against you. He will say to you thus: The acts which you call mine are not mine. I am a mere machine in the matter, and what appears to be my actions are not really mine, but the results of laws that I cannot avoid or escape. As the law which makes me act is the guilty party, let the law suffer the consequences. Why should the law compel me to act and then leave *me* to suffer? Why tell me to stop doing bad after placing me under a law that robs me of all liberty, of all freedom of action? I may be bad, but I am not a fool. I may be bad because I murdered a man, but I am no worse than the guillotine that has killed more than I have and is as free as I am; it, like me, is governed by a law or a force above and independent of it. Why should it not suffer as well as I? Give me no more of your advice. Reserve it for the guillotine, the noose, and the electric chair. I will go on obeying the law I cannot disobey, and the so-called badness or goodness of acts which you inconsistently call mine must be attributed to the unavoidable law that compels me to act; and if I must suffer the consequences of acts I am not free not to do, then I must suffer them, but do not add to my sufferings by mocking me with your advice. I do not want to suffer before my time.

Ingersoll.— If it be a fact in nature that all must reap what they sow, there is neither mercy nor cruelty in this fact and I hold no God responsible for it.

Lambert.— But it is not a fact if there be no Supreme Intelligence to distinguish between good and bad acts, and no Supreme Power to reward the one and punish the other. It is in view of the existence of this Supreme, All-powerful Being that the Christian says: "As you sow so shall you reap." But you who deny the existence of this Being have no ground whatever for affirming that we shall reap as we sow. Blind nature cannot distinguish between good and bad, moral and immoral acts. There is no moral good or bad in physical causes and effects. Morality or immorality can be affirmed only of the moral order, of the acts of moral agents. And of these acts nature can take no cognizance and hence cannot be a judge to determine and execute the consequences. The purely physical part of an act of theft is neither good nor bad, and hence can have no corresponding results. He whose hand is burned accidently, and he whose hand is burned intentionally suffer equal pain, for nature makes no distinction. She can see in an act of theft only the transfer of money from one man's pocket to that of another, and to her eyeless front there is nothing to distinguish an honest transfer from a dishonest one. She treats alike, him, down whose throat arsenic is forced, and him who takes it with the intention of suicide. He, then, who denies the existence of an all-wise Judge, who distinguishes the good from the evil intention of a moral free agent and rewards and punishes accordingly, talks nonsense when he says we shall reap what we sow. Much of Ingersoll's argument depends on the *apparent* agreement between him and the Christian in the dictum that "as we sow so shall we reap." But it is evident there is no real agreement. If by "nature" Ingersoll means this visible, material universe, nothing is more certain than that men do not reap what they sow. If by nature he means the whole scope of existence in time and eternity, the same physical laws will continue to work out their results and the innocent and guilty alike will continue to suffer for all eternity, just as we see they are doing now. There is no way to readjust things except to admit the existence of a Supreme Being, who can distinguish between the just and the wicked and intervene between the evil cause and its results.

Grant this Being and the Christian will admit that man reaps what he sows; deny Him and there is no truth in the saying.

Ingersoll.— There is neither mercy nor cruelty in this fact (that man must reap what he sows).

Lambert.— But as it is not a fact (without a Supreme Being) what have you to say? You must say nature is cruel or that it is an irresponsible creature of a Supreme Being who will in His own time see to it that good acts will be ultimately rewarded and evil ones punished if not repented of. Or, as you express it, good acts will have their good consequences and evil ones evil consequences, forever.

Ingersoll.— I hold no God responsible for it.

Lambert.— That is generous in you. It would be too bad if you took a notion to hold Him responsible.

Ingersoll.— The trouble with the Christian creed

is that God is described as the one Who gives rewards and the one Who inflicts eternal pain.

Lambert.— The trouble is only in your eye. You have told us that nature in inducing "consequences" is neither cruel nor merciful. Now it is difficult to see how the same "consequences" become cruel when induced by God and called punishments. As to eternal pain we have seen that it must follow from your own philosophy of materialism.

Ingersoll.— You must say to the bad: If you stop doing bad you need not increase your burdens.

Lambert.— But what of those things the bad have already done? In your philosophy there is no place for repentance, restitution or rehabilitation. For him who has done evil there is no turning back, nothing but to suffer the eternal consequences. No good he may do thereafter can change his fate. When we consider that even the just man falls, there is little consolation and no hope for the poor sinner. Your philosophy on this point is the Devil's gospel and you his prophet.

Ingersoll.— It is admitted that man must bear the consequences of his acts.

Lambert.— It is not admitted unless you admit the existence of the Supreme Being Who alone can make man bear the consequences of his acts, the

Being Who alone knows whether the acts deserve good or bad consequences.

Ingersoll.—If the consequences are good the acts are good.

Lambert.— We have talked of this before and have seen that your rule is practically worthless since (if there be no God) the consequences of acts can never be known.

Ingersoll.— If the consequences are bad the acts are bad.

Lambert.— We have seen in the case of the agnostic thief that *two sets of consequences* followed from his act, good consequences to him and his family, and bad consequences to the man from whom he stole the money. Now, which set of consequences is to determine the nature of the thief's act? If you are right the thief's act was both good and bad, as the consequences were both good and bad. This is against the principle of reason that we cannot affirm and deny at the same time the same thing in the same sense.

Ingersoll.— Through experience we find that certain acts tend to unhappiness and others to happiness.

Lambert.— Through whose experience? Happiness and unhappiness, like all other modes of being, to exist at all must exist in the individual. The happiness or unhappiness of a community or society is the happiness or unhappiness of the individual members of the society. The experience, then, which teaches the acts that tend to happiness must be individual experience. Now, individuals have different tastes, tendencies, desires and impulses, so that happiness to one would be unhappiness to another. Each individual, then, must learn by personal experience what tends to happiness for *him*. This is a necessary result if man has no higher mind than the human to teach him. From this it follows, according to your theory, that every man has the right to do every act that he is intellectually and physically able to do, until he learns by experience to distinguish those acts that tend to happiness from those that tend to unhappiness to *him*. There is no avoiding this conclusion, for all the experience of mankind cannot teach him what, with his peculiar character, constitution, tendencies and propensities, will tend to his personal happiness — and aside from personal happiness there is none. He stands out alone, in the vast solitude of his own personality, with his experiences and characteristics, for no two men were ever alike. Then, aside from the supernatural mind that knows him perfectly, there is nothing but his own personal experiences to teach him what tends to his happiness.

He, therefore, in the nature of the case, has the right to do every intellectual and physical act that he can do to experiment and find out what tends to his happiness. This is the logical conclusion from Ingersoll's doctrines. It is a revolting conclusion and the doctrine from which it is deduced is equally abhorrent. If there were libertines and outlaws enough to put it into practice and imbeciles enough in the world to permit it to be practiced, courts, laws, civilization and society would vanish, and man would have to take to the woods and seek protection among his more respectable relatives, the gibbering monkeys, in the shades of the forests. Man's evil propensities would have full excuse and encouragement, and the world would be a pandemonium of crime. But the world has not gone lunatic and Ingersoll's insane dreams will not prevail. History proves that experience does not teach man what tends to his happiness. The revealed will and law of the Supreme Being alone teaches man to know his true destiny and that his true happiness consists in the attainment of the end of his creation.

Ingersoll.— There is still another trouble.

Lambert.— Yes, the world is full of troubles. But tell us about this particular trouble.

Ingersoll.— This God, if infinite, must have

known when He created man exactly who would be eternally damned. What right had He to create man, knowing that he was to be damned?

Lambert.—The first thought that occurs here is that He Who has the power to create cannot be catechised by anything that He creates. You must admit that *to be*, *to exist*, is a good thing in itself. Therefore to cause things or persons to come into existence is a good thing. Then, the Supreme Being has a right to call into being by His creative act whomsoever and whatsoever He wills. No one can deny this who admits that existence is a good thing or a better thing than non-existence. When I speak of the *right* of the Supreme Being, I simply come down to your low plane of thought, for strictly speaking, the Supreme Being has no rights whatever, because He *is* THE RIGHT, the Source, Origin, and Measure of all rights. When we talk of rights we refer to relations between existences, creatures. But the Supreme Being is neither an existence nor a creature. He is simply the Being, necessary, eternal, infinite, the source of thought and of things. Having no equal, and being entirely unique, He bears no relation to anything, except that of cause, and things and thought bear no relation to Him except that of dependence. To talk, therefore, as you do, about His rights, is to make the finite intellect, groping as it is, in darkness, doubt and uncertainty, the measure of the infinite intellect, the source of existence, certainty and truth. A moment's reflection will show you how absurd this is. Now with this understanding we will discuss what you call the "rights" of God.

Existence being a good thing, God has the right to create existences. Intelligence being good, He has the right to create intelligences. Liberty being good,— you said in a recent lecture, "Liberty thou art my God,"— He can give liberty to intelligent existences. Then to create intelligent free existences is good. This settles the question of right. It is just here that comes in the *gravamen* of your question. How can the Supreme Being create intelligent, free existences when He knows that some of them will abuse their liberty and deliberately and with malice aforethought place causes that of their very nature lead to eternal painful consequences to the placer of those causes? The answer is very simple. It is this. Existence is a real good. Liberty is a real good. But existence and liberty make evil a possibility, a *mere possibility*, therefore the Supreme Being had a right to do a *real good* even though from that *real* good a *possible* evil might follow. This *possible* evil happened, you will say, but why did God permit it to happen? I reply that in giving His intelligent creatures liberty He had to include the possibility of its happening. He had to deny His intelligent creatures liberty or give it to them with the possibility of their abusing it. He elected to give it to them and hold them responsible for its abuse. But why create a man that He knew would abuse it? Because the *existence* of that man is in itself a good and will continue for eternity to be a good even though the man by his own act should make it miserable in reference to himself. His being is God's, his mode of future existence is his own.

CHAPTER VII.

Ingersoll.— The reverend gentleman (Rev. J. B. Hamilton) tells us again the story of the agonies endured by Thomas Paine when dying; tells us that he then said that he wished his works had been thrown into the fire, that he frequently asked the Lord Jesus to have mercy on him. Of course there is not a word of truth in the story.

Lambert.— The Rev. Mr. Hamilton has not been content to let you have the last word on this subject. In a letter published subsequently in the

Telegram, he adduces proof of his assertion. I will let him speak for himself.

Hamilton.— Stephen Greliet, the son of a French nobleman, who was proscribed by the French revolutionists, made his home in America. He was led from infidelity by the writings of William Penn and became a Quaker preacher and missionary. The spotless purity of his life, exalted nobility of his Christian character, make it impossible for him to be charged with misrepresentation or mis-statement. He says in his biography:—

"I may not omit recording here the death of Thomas Paine. A few days previous to my leaving home on my last religious visit, on hearing that he was ill and in a very destitute condition, I went to see him and found him in a wretched state, for he had been so neglected and forsaken by his pretended friends that the common attentions to a sick man had been withheld from him. The skin of his body was in some places worn off, which greatly increased his sufferings. A nurse was provided for him and some needful comforts were supplied. He was mostly in a state of stupor, and something that had passed between us had made such an impression upon him that some days after my departure he sent for me, and, on being told that I was gone from home he sent for another Friend.

"This induced a valuable young Friend (Mary Roscoe), who had resided in my family and continued at Greenwich during part of my absence, frequently to go and take him some little refreshment suitable for an invalid, furnished by a neighbor. Once when she was there, three of his deistical associates came to the door, and in a loud and unfeeling manner said: 'Tom Paine, it is said you are turning Christian, but we hope you will die as you have lived,' and then went away. On which, turning to Mary Roscoe, he said: 'You see what miserable comforters they are.'

"Once he asked her if she had ever read any of his writings, and on being told that she had read but very little of them, he inquired what she thought of them, adding, 'From such a one as you I expect a correct answer.' She told him that when very young his 'Age of Reason' was put into her hands, but that the more she read in it the more dark and distressed she felt, and she threw the book into the fire. 'I wish all had done as you,' he replied, 'for if the Devil has ever had any agency in any work he has had it in my writing that book.' When going to carry him some refreshment, she repeatedly heard him uttering the language, 'O Lord!' or 'Lord Jesus, have mercy upon me.'"

Lambert.— To this I will add the testimony of Dr. Manly, Paine's physician. This witness says:—

"During the latter part of his life, though his conversation was equivocal, his conduct was singular. He would not be left alone, night or day. He not only required to have some person with him, but he must see that he or she was there and would not allow his curtain to be closed at any time. And if, as sometimes would unavoidably happen, he was left alone, he would scream and halloo until some one came to him. When relief from pain would admit, he seemed thoughtful and contemplative, his eyes being generally closed, and his hands folded upon his breast, though he never slept without the assistance of an anodyne. There was something remarkable in his conduct about this period (which comprises two weeks immediately preceding his death) particularly when we reflect that Thomas Paine was the author of the 'Age of Reason.' He would call out during the paroxysms of his distress without intermission, ' *O Lord, help me! God help me! Jesus Christ, help me, Lord help me,*' etc., repeating the same expression without any variation, in a tone of voice that would alarm the house.

"I took occasion, during the night of the 5th of June, to test the strength of his opinions respecting Revelation. I purposely made him a very late visit. It was at a time that seemed to suit exactly with my errand. It was midnight. He was in great distress, constantly exclaiming in the words above mentioned; when, after a considerable preface, I addressed him in the following manner, the nurse being present: 'Mr. Paine, your opinions, by a large portion of the community, have been treated with deference. You have never been in the habit of mixing in your conversation words of cursing. You have never indulged in the practice of profane swearing, you must be sensible that we are acquainted with your religious opinions as they are given to the world. What must we think of your present conduct? Why do you call upon Jesus Christ to help you? Do you believe in the divinity of Jesus Christ? Come now, answer me honestly. I want an answer from the lips of a dying man, for I verily believe you will not live twenty-four hours.' I waited for some time at the end of every question; he did not answer, but ceased to exclaim in the above manner. Again I addressed him: 'Mr. Paine, you have not answered my questions; will you answer them? Allow me to ask again, do you believe, or let me qualify the question, do you wish to believe, that Jesus Christ is the son of God?' After a pause of some minutes, he answered, 'I have no wish to believe on that subject.' I then left him, and know not whether he afterwards spoke to any person on any subject, though he lived, as I before observed, to the morning of the 8th of June."

To this testimony as to Paine's state of mind, I will add that of the Rt. Rev. Edward Fenwick, first Catholic Bishop of Cincinnati. He says:—

"A short time before Paine died, I was sent for by him. I was accompanied by F. Kohlman, an intimate friend. We found him at a house in Greenwich (not Greenwich street, New York), where he lodged. A decent looking elderly woman came to the door, and inquired whether we were the Catholic priests; 'For' said she, 'Mr. Paine has been so much annoyed of late by other denominations calling upon him, that he has left express orders to admit no one but the clergymen of the Catholic Church.' Upon informing her who we were, she opened a door and showed us into the parlor. . . 'Gentlemen,' said the lady, 'I really wish you may succeed with Mr. Paine, for he is laboring under great distress of mind ever since he was told by his physician that he cannot possibly live, and must die shortly. He is truly to be pitied. His cries when left alone are heart-rending. "O Lord, help me!" he will exclaim, during his paroxysms of distress; "God, help me; Jesus Christ, help me!"—repeating these words in a tone of voice that would alarm the house. Sometimes he will say, "O God, what have I done to suffer so much?" Then shortly after, "But there is no God;" and then again, "Yet if there should be, what would become of me hereafter?" Thus he will continue for some time, when, on a sudden, he will scream as if in terror and agony, and call for me by name. On one occasion I inquired what he wanted. "Stay with me," he replied, "for God's sake! for I cannot bear to be left alone." I told him I could not always be in the room. "*Then*," said he, "*send even a child to stay with me, for it is a hell to be alone.*"' '*I never saw,*' said she, '*a more unhappy, a more forsaken, man. It seems he cannot reconcile himself to die.*'

"Such was the conversation of the woman, who was a Protestant, and who seemed very desirous that we should afford him some relief in a state bordering on complete despair. Having remained some time in the parlor, we at length heard a noise in the adjoining room. We proposed to enter; which was assented to by the woman, who opened the door for us. *A more wretched being in appearance I never beheld. He was lying on a bed sufficiently decent in itself, but at present besmeared* with filth; his look was that of a man greatly tortured in mind, his eyes haggard; his countenance forbidding and his whole appearance that of one whose better days had been but one continued scene of debauch.* His only nourishment was milk punch, in which he indulged to the full extent of his weak state. He had partaken very recently of it, as the sides and corners of his mouth exhibited very unequivocal traces of it, as well as of blood which had followed in the track and left its mark on the pillow. Upon their making known the object of their visit, Paine interrupted the speaker by saying, 'That's enough, sir, that's enough. I see what you would be about. I wish to hear no more of you, sir; my mind is made up on that subject. I look upon the whole Christian scheme to be a tissue of lies, and Jesus Christ to be nothing more than a cunning knave and impostor. Away with you and your God, too! leave the room instantly! All that you have uttered are lies, filthy lies and if I had a little more time I would prove it, as I did about your impostor, Jesus Christ.' Among the last utterances that fell upon the ears of the attendants of this dying infidel, and which have been recorded in history, were the words, 'My God, my God, why hast thou forsaken me?'

Ingersoll.— As to the personal habits of Mr.

Paine we have the testimony of William Carver, with whom he lived.

Lambert.— It was a strange infatuation that led you to refer to William Carver for a character of Tom Paine. As he is one of your own witnesses his testimony is unimpeachable. In a letter to Paine, dated December 2, 1806, and published in the *New York Observer*, November, 1, 1877, William Carver wrote as follows:—

"A respectable gentleman from New Rochelle called to see me a few days back, and said that everybody was tired of you there, and that no one would undertake to board and lodge you. I thought this was the case, as I found you at a tavern in a most miserable situation. You appeared as if you had not been shaved for a fortnight, and as to a shirt, it could not be said that you had one on — it was only the remains of one — and this likewise appeared not to have been off your back for a fortnight, and was nearly the color of tanned leather; and you had *the most disagreeable smell possible*— just like that of our poor beggars in England. Do you remember the pains I took to clean you? that I got a tub of warm water and soap, and washed you from head to foot, and this I had to do three times before I could get you clean? You say also that you found your own liquors during the time you boarded with me; but you should have said, 'I found only a small part of the liquor I drank during my stay with you; this part I purchased of John Fellows, which was a demijohn of brandy, containing four gallons, and this did not serve me three weeks.' This can be proved, and I mean not to say anything I cannot prove, for I hold truth as a precious jewel. It is a well-known fact that you drank one quart of brandy per day, at my expense, during the different times that you boarded with me, and the last fourteen weeks you were sick. Is not this a supply of liquor for dinner and supper? Now, sir, I think I have drawn a complete portrait of your character; yet to enter into every minutia, would be to give a history of your life, and to develop the fallacious mask of hypocrisy and deception under which you have acted in your political as well as moral capacity of life."

It must have been Poe's Angel of the Odd that inspired you to call in William Carver as a witness in behalf of Paine.

The historian Hildreth thus sums up the character of Paine. After quoting an abusive article from the *Aurora* newspaper, in which Washington was accused of the "foulest designs against the liberties of the people." Hildreth adds : —

"This, indeed, was but a somewhat exaggerated

specimen of the abusive articles to be found almost daily in the columns of the *Aurora*, from the office of which had just issued *a most virulent pamphlet*, under the form of a letter to Washington from the notorious Thomas Paine, whose natural insolence and dogmatism had become aggravated by *habitual drunkenness*."

Again, this same historian says: " Paine, instead of being esteemed as formerly, as a lover of liberty, whose vigorous pen had hastened the Declaration of Independence, was now detested by large numbers *as the libeler of Washington*."

Ingersoll.— He (Paine) was the first to advocate separation from the mother country.

Lambert.— This is not true. Paine himself says, in his pamphlet called " Common Sense: " "All men, whether in England or America, confess that separation between the two countries will take place one time or another."

Franklin, before Paine's pamphlet was published, wrote to a friend in Holland, that "American independence is likely to be declared before long." It was at Franklin's suggestion that Paine wrote his pamphlet.

Samuel Adams had said in the Massachusetts Assembly: " The Declaration of Independence and treaties with foreign powers are to be expected."

Paine's pamphlet was published *anonymously* — a plan to save his neck in case of the failure of the cause — in January, 1776. Now, on the 31st of May, 1775, the committee of Mecklenburg County, North Carolina, met and adopted the following resolutions : —

"They (the committee) conceive that all laws and commissions confirmed by or derived from the authority of the King and Parliament, are annulled and vacated, and the former civil constitution of these colonies for the present wholly suspended." The first resolution declares all commissions granted by the crown to be void. The second declares that no *legislative or executive power exists, except in the provincial congress of each province.* The sixteenth declares that "whatever person shall hereafter receive a commission from the crown, or attempt to exercise any such commission heretofore received, shall be deemed an enemy to the country."

Yet in the face of all this, Mr. Ingersoll has the supreme effrontery to tell his audience that Paine "was the first to advocate separation from the mother country." Was he ignorant of the facts, or did he count on the ignorance of his audience?

Ingersoll.— Paine's "Common Sense" was the first argument for separation.

Lambert.— This is not true. There were several arguments for separation in the shape of the battles of Lexington, Concord, Bunker Hill and Quebec. "Before Paine had set foot on our soil, our revolutionary sires had gone so far that they were compelled to go further. Before them was success as heroes or death as traitors. There was no retreat. Their necks were in the halter before they heard that such a man as Paine ever lived." (W. H. Platt).

Ingersoll.— The moment he (Paine) died, the pious commenced manufacturing horrors for his deathbed. They had his chamber filled with devils rattling chains.

Lambert.— When we consider that he swilled into himself four gallons of brandy in less than three weeks, according to William Carver with whom he lodged, it is not surprising that he saw strange things and wished not to be left alone for a moment. It is possible that the "pious," in their ignorance, misinterpreted these symptoms and imagined supernatural causes when there were only natural effects. The modern physician would attribute the symptoms to *mania potu* or *delirium tremens*.

Ingersoll.— A couple of Catholic priests, in all the meekness of arrogance, called that they might enjoy the agonies of the dying friend of man.

Lambert.— Bishop Fenwick, one of the priests you refer to, wrote an account of this visit in which he says: "*A short time before Paine died, I was sent for by him.*" So what you say of him and his friend is in the arrogance of mendacity.

You may ask why do I drag these disreputable habits of Paine from obscurity? Why not exercise Christian charity and leave the dead to the silence of the grave and to the judgment of his Creator? It is because you go about the country attempting to canonize him and raise him up above the brave and good Christian men, who, by their courage and patriotism, achieved our independence. It is because in your laudations of this seducer of another man's wife, this libeler of Washington, you leave no opportunity pass to insult Christian sentiment, to defame and degrade those witnesses whose evidence does not tell in his favor.

It is because you malign the characters of those Christian ministers who treated a coarse blasphemer with the contempt he deserved. You complain that he was forsaken by those he helped to free. But why should they continue to honor a man who persisted in insulting, degrading and dishonoring that which was dearer to them than life — their religion? Your political hopes have been forever blasted by the same conduct, and you must not expect a Christian people to condone it as long as you persist. It is possible that much of your bitterness against the Christian religion is the bitterness of a disappointed career.

The story is told that you were once traveling in Illinois and talking as usual about the Bible. An old Methodist lady who heard you said: "Well, Mr. Ingersoll, the Bible did one good thing at least." "What was that, madame?" "It prevented you from being governor of Illinois." That old lady struck the key of your anti-Christian bitterness, which you would call zeal for truth, liberty, enlightenment, but that is mere poetry and deceives nobody. Your friends sought recognition of your political services, but no administration could carry you and survive. This would seem to prove that Christianity is not quite as dead as you imagine.

Before leaving Paine I will quote Franklin's letter to him in which he tries to dissuade him from publishing his "Age of Reason." It is a letter you could meditate on with advantage. You will find it in Niles' "Register," vol. XXX., page 397.

"DEAR SIR:—I have read your manuscript with some attention. By the argument it contains against a particular Providence, though you allow a general Providence, you strike at the foundation of all religion. For without the belief of a Providence, that takes cognizance of, guards and guides, and favors particular persons, there is no motive to worship a Deity, to fear its displeasure, or to pray for its protection. I will not enter into any discussion of your principles, though you seem to desire it. At present I shall only give you my opinion, that though your reasonings are subtle, and may prevail with some readers, you will not succeed so as to change the general sentiment of mankind on that subject; and the consequence of printing this piece will be a great deal of odium upon yourself, mischief to you, and no good to others. He that spits against the wind spits in his own face. But were you to succeed, do you imagine any good will be done by it? You yourself may find it easy to live a virtuous life without the assistance afforded by religion. You have a clear perception of the advantages of virtue, and the disadvantages of vice, and possess strength of resolution sufficient to enable you to resist common temptations. But think how great a portion of mankind consists of ignorant men and women, and of inexperienced, inconsiderate youth, of both sexes, who have need of the motives of religion to restrain them from vice, to support their virtue, and retain them in the practice of it until it becomes *habitual*, which is the great point for its security. And, perhaps, you are indebted to her originally, that is to your religious education, for the habits of virtue upon which you now justly value yourself. You might easily display your excellent talents of reasoning upon a less hazardous subject and thereby obtain rank among our most distinguished authors. For among us it is not necessary, as among the Hottentots, that a youth to be raised into the company of men should prove his manhood by beating his mother. I should advise you, therefore, not to attempt unchaining the tiger, but to burn this piece before it is seen by any other person, whereby you will save yourself a great deal of mortification from the enemies it may raise against you, and perhaps a good deal of regret and repentance. If men are so wicked *with* religion, what would they be without it? I intend this letter itself as a proof of my friendship, and therefore add no profession, but simply subscribe,

Yours,
B. Franklin.'

Ingersoll.— Let me tell you how Voltaire died.
Lambert.— Well go on so that we can see how

much truth you can tell on that interesting subject.

Ingersoll.— Towards the end of May, 1788, it was whispered in Paris that Voltaire was dying.

Lambert.— This was indeed strange as Voltaire was dead and buried ten years before that date. You should incorporate your statement in your lecture on myths or ghosts, for it must have been only the ghost of a whisper. You are a great stickler for "facts," and call them legal tender, yet in telling when Voltaire died you came within ten years of it; but that is, after all, a pretty fair average for you, and a small trifle like that is nothing. You, no doubt, gave your "honest thought" on the subject. At first I honestly thought it was a typographical blunder perpetrated by the printer's devil, but a few lines further on I found you repeated the same date — less one year — and quote Wagniere as your authority. Now, as you blunder so egregiously about *when* he died, what confidence can be placed in you when you undertake to tell *how* he died? Let me give you an easy mathematical problem in the Rule of Three. If a man makes a blunder of ten years in fixing the date of an event that happened one hundred and fourteen years ago, how many years would he lose or gain in fixing the date of events that took place four or five thousand years ago? and what would his authority be worth in discussing the chronology of Moses?

Having given your honest thought as to *when* Voltaire died, we are ready to hear some of your story as to the *manner* of his death.

Ingersoll.— Upon the fences of expectation gathered the unclean birds of superstition, impatiently waiting for their prey.

Lambert.— There, now, enough of that. That's only poetry. Do not let those " unclean birds " distract your attention from the main drift of your story.

Ingersoll.— Two day before his death, his nephew went to seek the Curé of St. Sulpice and the Abbé Gautier, and brought them into his uncle's sick chamber, who was then informed that they were there. "Ah, well," said Voltaire, "give them my compliments and my thanks."

Lambert.— You state this in such a way as to leave the impression that the coming of the priests was the result of the pious zeal of his nephew and not at the solicitation of Voltaire himself. The following letter explains the presence of the priests at Voltaire's bedside : —

" You have promised me, sir, to come to hear me. I entreat you would take the trouble of calling on me as soon as possible. Signed: VOLTAIRE, Paris, 26th of February, 1778."

Now, "honor bright," why did you suppress this letter? If you did not know of its existence, you are too ignorant to undertake to give an account of the manner of Voltaire's death, and if you knew of its existence and had not the "courage of the soul" to give it, what are we to think of you? Go on.

Ingersoll.— The Abbé spoke some words to Voltaire, exhorting him to patience. The Curé of St. Sulpice then came forward, having announced himself, and asked Voltaire, lifting his voice, if he acknowledged the divinity of our Lord Jesus Christ. The sick man pushed one of his hands against the Curé's coif, shoving him back and cried, turning abruptly to the other side: "Let me die in peace."

The Curé seemingly considered his person soiled and his coif dishonored by the touch of the philosopher. He made the nurse give him a little brushing and went out with the Abbé Gautier.

Lambert.— This Abbé's name was Gaultier and not Gautier as you repeat it. But amid your accumulation of blunders this is a small matter. We can make out what you mean.

It should have occurred to you that the Abbé might have had other reasons than the "touch of the philosopher" for having the nurse give him a little brushing. The French Abbé is proverbially a neat and cleanly person.

Ingersoll.— "He expired," says Wagniere, "on May 30," 1787, at about a quarter past eleven o'clock at night, with the most perfect tranquillity.

Lambert.— How exceedingly minute this writer is about the time, after having made a blunder of nine years as to the date — as quoted by Ingersoll.

Now as to Voltaire's death and the circumstances attending it. On February 5, 1778, he left Ferney, where he had resided for many years, and arrived in Paris on the 10th, at the age of eighty-four years. About a fortnight after his arrival, he became seriously ill and sent for a confessor, as appears from the following letter to the Abbé Gaultier, which as it is short I will requote:—

"You have promised me, sir, to come to hear me. I entreat you would take the trouble of calling on me as soon as possible. Signed: VOLTAIRE, Paris, the 26th of February, 1778."

As a result of this interview with the Abbé, and six days after the date of the above letter, he wrote the following declaration in the presence of the Abbé Gaultier, the Abbé Mignot, and the Marquis de Villevieille, which is copied from the minutes deposited with M. Momet, notary at Paris:—

"I, the underwritten, declare, that for these four

days past, having been afflicted with a vomiting of blood, at the age of eighty-four, and not having been able to drag myself to the Church, the Rev. the rector of St. Sulpice, having been pleased to add to his good works, that of sending to me the Abbé Gaultier, I confessed to him, and if it please God to dispose of me, I die in the Church in which I was born,* hoping that the divine mercy will pardon all my faults. Second of March, 1778. Signed VOLTAIRE, in the presence of Abbé Mignot my nephew, and the Marquis de Villevieille, my friend."

Now, again, I ask, why, in giving an account of Voltaire's mental state, previous to his death, did you suppress this important document?

After the witnesses had signed this declaration, Voltaire added these words, which are copied from the same minutes in possession of M. Momet, notary at Paris:

"The Abbé Gaultier, my confessor, having apprised me, that it was said among a certain set of people 'that I should protest against anything I did at my death;' I declare that I never made such a speech, and that it is an old jest, attributed long since to many of the learned, more enlightened than I am."

---

* The Catholic Church.

This declaration is also signed by the Marquis de Villevieille, the same to whom, eleven years before, Voltaire wrote, "Conceal your march from the enemy, in your endeavors to *crush the wretch*," words with which he closed many of his letters to his infidel friends.

He permitted the above declaration to be carried to the Rector of St. Sulpice and to the Archbishop of Paris to know whether it would be sufficient.

After having thus purged himself and relieved his guilty mind, he recovered sufficiently to busy himself about his affairs, and, like the consummate hypocrite he was all his life, he scoffed at himself as usual. In the latter part of May he relapsed, and to quote from the "Encyclopædia Britannica:" "On May 30 the priests were once more sent for, to wit, his nephew the Abbé Mignot, the Abbé Gaultier, who had officiated on the former occasion, and the parish priest, the Curé of St. Sulpice. He was, however, in a state of half insensibility, and petulantly motioned them away."

The Abbé Gaultier signed a paper in which he declared that he was sent for at the request of Voltaire, but found him too far gone to confess. He died on May 30, 1778, not 1788, as you ignorantly assert.

The Curé of St. Sulpice refused to inter the

body and it was taken to the Abbey of Scellieres, where, on the presentation of the declaration of the second of March (given above), it was buried.

I make the following quotation descriptive of the scenes at his deathbed from "Letters of Certain Jews to Voltaire," appendix page 596.

"D'Alembert, Diderot, and about twenty others of the conspirators who had beset his apartment, never approached him but to witness their own ignominy, and often he would curse them and exclaim: 'Retire, it is you that have brought me to my present state! Begone! I could have done without you all; but you could not exist without me! And what a wretched glory you have procured me!' Then would succeed the horrid remembrance of his conspiracy. They could hear him the prey of anguish and dread, alternately supplicating or blaspheming that God against whom he had conspired; and in plaintive accents would he cry out, 'Oh, Christ! Oh, Jesus Christ!' And then complain that he was abandoned by God and man. The hand which had traced in ancient writ the sentence of an impious and reviling King seemed to trace before his eyes, 'Crush them, do crush the wretch.' In vain he turned his head away; the time was coming apace when he was to appear before the tribunal of Him whom he had blasphemed, and his physicians, particularly M. Tronchin, called to administer relief, retired thunderstruck, declaring the death of the impious man to be terrible indeed. The pride of the conspirators would willingly have suppressed these declarations, but it was in vain. The Mareschal de Richelieu fled from the bedside declaring it to be a sight too terrible to be sustained; and M. Tronchin, that the furies of Orestes could give but a faint idea of those of Voltaire."

This account of the unhappy end of Voltaire is confirmed by a letter of M. de Luc, an eminent philosopher, and man of the strictest honor and probity.

As there is nothing worthy of attention in the remainder of Ingersoll's *Telegram* article, we will take a recess here till his next outbreak.

THE END.

www.ingramcontent.com/pod-product-compliance
Lightning Source LLC
Chambersburg PA
CBHW031833230426
43669CB00009B/1326